THE
CHURCH-
IDEA

LIBRARY OF EPISCOPALIAN CLASSICS

THE CHURCH-IDEA

An Essay Towards Unity

William Reed Huntington, D.D.
Late Rector of Grace Church in New York

MOREHOUSE PUBLISHING

Harrisburg, PA

© 2002 Morehouse Publishing

Morehouse Publishing
P.O. Box 1321
Harrisburg, PA 17105

Morehouse Publishing is a division of The Morehouse Group.

Cover design by Corey Kent

This work was previously published
1870 © E.P. Dutton and Company
1899 © C. Scribner's Sons
1928 © Houghton Mifflin Company

The opinions expressed in this book are solely those of the author, who originally published *The Church-Idea* in 1870. His thoughts on race and religion reflect his times, and are not intended to offend any religious or racial group nor to reflect the current teachings of the Episcopal Church.

Library of Congress Cataloging-in-Publication Data

Huntington, William Reed, 1838-1909
    The Church-idea : an essay towards unity /
by William Reed Huntington.
        p. cm.
    Originally published: Boston ; New York : Houghton Mifflin, 1928.
    Includes bibliographical references.
    ISBN 0-8192-1913-4 (alk. paper)
    1. Christian union   I. Title.
    BX8.3 .H86 2002
    262'.001'1—dc21   2001004523

Printed in the United States of America

02 03 04 05 06 07 08 09   9 8 7 6 5 3 2 1

Contents

I. The Gospel of the Kingdom

DISSATISFACTION is the one word that best expresses the state of mind in which Christendom finds itself today. There is a wide-spread misgiving that we are on the eve of momentous changes. Unrest is everywhere. The party of the Curia and the party of the Reformation, the party of orthodoxy and the party of liberalism, are all alike agitated by the consciousness that a spirit of change is in the air.

No wonder that many imagine themselves listening to the rumbling of the chariot-wheels of the Son of Man. He Himself predicted that "perplexity" should be one of the signs of his coming, and it is certain that breads of the social order have seldom been more intricately entangled than they now are.

A calmer and perhaps truer inference is that we are about to enter on a new reach of Church history, and that the dissatisfaction and perplexity are only transient. There is always a tumult of waves at the meeting of the waters; but when the streams have mingled, the flow is smooth and still again. The plash and gurgle that we hear may mean something like this.

At all events the time is opportune for a discussion of the Church-Idea; for it is with this, hidden under a hundred disguises, that the world's thoughts are busy. Men have become possessed with an unwonted longing for unity, and yet they are aware that they do not grapple successfully with the practical problem. Somehow they are grown persuaded that union is God's work, and separation devil's work; but the persuasion only breeds the greater discontent. That is what lies at the root of our unquietness. There is a felt want and a felt inability to meet the want; and where these two things coexist there must be heat of friction.

Catholicity is what we are reaching after. But how is Catholicity to be defined? And when we have got our definition, what are we to do with it? The speculative and the practical sides of the question are about equally difficult to meet. The humanitarian scheme would make the Church conterminous with the race; the ultramontane would bound it by the Papal decrees.

Clearly we have come upon a time for the study of first principles, a time to go down and look after the foundations upon which our customary beliefs are built. The more searching the analysis, the more lasting will the synthesis be sure to be.

The present papers presuppose in the reader a certain amount of Christian faith, enough, at least, to give him a general interest in the subject under review. They do not, however, take for granted any definite conclusions as to the nature or intent of the Christian Church. We will begin, therefore, at the beginning, with the Church-Idea itself.

And first of all this very expression must be justified. What is the Church-Idea ?

Briefly it is this, that the Son of God came down from heaven to be the Savior not only of men, but of man; to bring "good tidings of great joy" not only to every separate soul, but also to all souls collectively. He died, not only to save the scattered sheep, but to gather them that they might be *scattered* sheep no longer. If we would receive the Gospel in its fullness, we must recognize it as a message endowed with a twofold significance, sent with a twofold purpose, freighted with a twofold blessing.

Not that there are two Gospels—God forbid! St. Paul would have his Galatians hold accursed even the angel who shall dare to preach to them a second Gospel. But this single Gospel has a twofold outlook; in the one direction it fronts upon the individual, in the other it fronts upon society.[1]

Every man that breathes has his own personal need of pardon at God's hands. The Gospel meets him with its promise of forgiveness. Again, the great family of men, as a family, asks to be reconciled and set in order. The Gospel meets this want with its announcement of a Kingdom organized upon the principle of holiness.

"The Gospel" ought to be regarded as the entire blessing resulting to the world from the birth, life, death, resurrection, and ascension of our Lord Jesus Christ. In this aggregate of blessing, the interests both of the one and of the many have a place. It is an injury to the balance of truth when either aspect is dwelt upon to the exclusion of the other. Many a weary estrangement in religion owes its origin to this mistake. If, in a rough way, we define the error of Romanism to be an overestimate of the value of organized Christianity, we ought also to admit that the error of Protestantism has lain in an underestimate of the same. The one theology tends to sacrifice the individual to the Church; the other tends to sacrifice the Church to the individual.

But we shall come to "the Roman Question" by and by. At present we are concerned with the abstract Church-Idea, and in determining whether it has, or has not, any intimate relation with the Gospel of Christ.

A glance at the very first instance in which the word "Gospel" occurs in the New Testament will give us light upon this point. The Evangelist St. Matthew tells us, in one of his earlier chapters, that as soon as our Lord's ministry was fairly begun, He "went about all Galilee teaching in their synagogues, and preaching the Gospel of the Kingdom."[2] Now we know what "Gospel" means, and we know what "Kingdom" means. Gospel is good news. A kingdom is one of the familiar forms of organized society. When, therefore, we are told that Jesus preached "the Gospel of the Kingdom," the natural and straightforward inference from the statement would seem to be that He announced to the people the coming of a new and better social order. It will be remembered that this had been the keynote also of the Baptist's cry in the desert. He had bidden men repent and be ready, because there was a kingdom close at hand. When the King came, his first utterance was but the amplification of what his harbinger had said. He also preached "the Gospel of the Kingdom."

But we are not left wholly to our own devices in searching out the meaning of this phrase. We have even better evidence than that of the ordinary laws of language. The discourses spoken in those Galilean synagogues and elsewhere on mountain, lake, and plain, are largely preserved to us. In sermon and parable we have the outline of the new Kingdom sketched, and so sketched as to persuade us that it is meant to be a thing very tangible and real. The impression given is that of a new society about to be established here on earth, a regenerate social order, that shall dwell within the older order, while yet wholly independent of it, the one community bearing to the other the relation that the embryo butterfly sustains to the larva it inhabits. There is to be brought in among the kingdoms of this world a Divine polity fruitful of change and sure of triumph; a polity that shall fulfill the promise of the *Magnificent,* putting down the mighty from their seats, exalting them of low degree; filling the hungry with good things, and sending the rich empty away.

But how does all this square with the ordinary definitions of "the Gospel"? To the question, What is the

Gospel? the usual answer would be something like this: "The Gospel is the blessed promise of pardon through the blood of Christ. It is the assurance that for me the Savior died." A true answer, doubtless; but is it the whole truth? Can it be the whole truth? Is this the Gospel that was preached by Jesus Christ in his own person?

Manifestly if the benefits of Christ's death were preached by Him while He was yet treading the soil of Palestine, and before He suffered, they must have been preached prophetically. But do we find this to have been the case? Do we discover in his recorded discourses very plentiful allusions to the Preacher's coming sacrifice of Himself? We certainly do find mysterious hints of what is to be wrought upon the Cross. Calvary looms heavily as we approach the close of the Gospel story. But do we find in the reported sayings of our Lord anything like the same prominence given to the distinctive doctrine of his sacrificial death that we find in the writings of the Apostles? Waiving for the moment those intimations and foreshadowings of a truth more fully to be revealed, do we discover among the words of Jesus any such plain, direct statement as this, for example, "The blood of Jesus Christ, His Son, cleanseth us from all sin"? No one, whatever his theological bias, will assert that we do. And yet "the Gospel" was preached even while

> "The Word had flesh, and wrought
> With human hands the creed of creeds."

The Gospel was preached then, for we are expressly told that it was, and it was Jesus Christ Himself who preached it. He, if anyone, must have known what the Gospel meant. And how did He preach the Gospel? The Evangelists tell us. Their record makes it plain, that, from the beginning of his preaching and teaching, Jesus presented his Gospel in the twofold aspect that has here been claimed for it. He taught the duty of personal allegiance to Himself. "Follow me," He said. That was the side of the Gospel that fronted on the individual. Again, He spoke repeatedly to his disciples of "the things pertaining to the Kingdom of God." That was the side of the Gospel that fronted upon society.

It is to be observed that neither one of these two bearings was clearly discerned until after the Savior's death. It was only when Pentecost had completed the cycle of the redemptive work that the "salvation which, at the first, began to be spoken by the Lord" could be either taught or received in its completeness.[3] The death and resurrection of the Gospel-bringer threw a flood of light upon what He had said about his kingly claims. Men began to see why so large a measure of personal loyalty was demanded of them, when they were shown how He who asked it had died to take away their sin. And they began to understand what was meant by the Gospel of a Kingdom, when they saw rising everywhere about them the walls and turrets of the new-founded City of God.

It will be seen that the writer's view identifies "the Kingdom" with the institution known in history as the Christian Church.

Against such an identification of the Kingdom with the Church, two arguments may be brought. The two are independent of each other, and, to a certain extent, in conflict; but since each has found distinguished as well as numerous upholders, it will be worth our while to examine them with carefulness.

The first of these two negative arguments may be compactly stated thus: Christ's Kingdom means his spiritual supremacy in the hearts of his several followers. It is not, and its Founder never intended it to be, a visible organization. The second is this: Christ's Kingdom means that coming down of the heavenly Jerusalem to earth, which we are to look for when the present order of the world passes away.

Of these arguments, the first supposes that the Kingdom has been already started in the world, but is invisible; the second holds that the Kingdom will be visible when it comes, but that it has not yet come. There is truth in both views. There is Scripture in support of both. Their error lies in their one-sidedness. The larger doctrine that is to include both must set forth a Kingdom at once visible and invisible, present and future.

Let us first look at the argument for invisibility. It is undeniable that the phrase "Kingdom of Heaven," or "Kingdom of God," admits of a subjective as well as an objective interpretation. Christ Himself says, "The Kingdom of God is within you,"[4] and this word of his has been the main reliance of the "invisible" hypothesis. But, when we think of it, every kingdom is, in one sense, "within" men. The essence of a kingdom does not lie in thrones, and crowns, and sceptres, and palaces, but in the king's consciousness of rightful authority, and in the people's consciousness of an obligation to obey. The true kingdom is "within" the subjects' hearts. And yet for all this, kingdoms, as we know them, are very real and visible things. Granting that Christ meant his Kingdom to be inward, does it follow that He did not mean it to be outward also? In such a discussion, the burden of proof rests upon those who deny the outwardness or visibility, not upon those who affirm it.

The Apostles are commonly believed to have known the mind of Christ as well, at least, as most modern theologians, and they certainly could not, after Pentecost, be called unspiritual men; yet these Apostles went forth from their forty days of intercourse with the risen Lord, and built up all over the world a society as visible and tangible as it well could be. This society had its terms of membership, its officers, its laws, its sacramental observances, its rites and usages. Long before the books of the New Testament had been gathered into a volume, the existence of this society was as real and evident to the eyes of men as that of the Roman Empire itself. There was nothing shadowy or uncertain about it. It was actual. It had a name. That name was The Church. This point will be more fully brought out later on; just now it is merely noted as a formidable fact in the way of those who would disprove Christ's intention of founding a visible Kingdom.

The parables of our Lord hold a very interesting relation to this question. They are almost all of them concerned with the nature of the Kingdom of Heaven; and it is a significant fact that while some of them are most readily interpreted of that Kingdom which is "within," and some of that which is "without," there are yet others that admit with equal ease of either interpretation.

Every student of the parables must have noticed this. Indeed, it is but another illustration of that law of duality which, as we have seen, runs through the whole system of revelation. The very fact that these symbolic sayings are illustrative of the Gospel causes them to partake of the Gospel's twofold character. Take, for example, the Parable of the Mustard Seed. We may understand it of God's truth sown in the heart of the believer and growing up into what we call ripe character, a tree beautiful in foliage and vocal with the song of birds. Or we may understand it of the seed of the new social order sown in the world, and springing up into a tree whose branches reach out over all lands, and whose top touches the sky. Either interpretation is beautiful, and probably both were intended.

The old philosophers were fond of calling man a microcosm, or little world in himself. So the Christian may be a little Kingdom of Heaven in himself. But as the microcosm does not exclude the macrocosm, the little world and the great world being admirably adjusted to each other, so neither does this double aspect of the parables at all impair their meaning.

The variety of limestone known as calc-spar crystallizes in the rhombohedral form. It is a peculiarity of this mineral that if you shatter a crystal of it by a blow of the hammer, each little fragment will be found to be a perfect rhombohedron in miniature. All that was true geometrically of the planes and axes and angles of the large crystal is also true of the planes and axes and angles of the tiny one. The same scientific formula that described the unbroken, mineral answers equally well for any fractured part. The only difference is in respect of magnitude. Let us interpret this parable of stone. It shows us that law of spiritual proportion may be applicable to the individual man, and yet not for this reason inapplicable to the "colossal man," society. It indicates also what is the right answer to those who would oppose the spirituality of the Kingdom to its visibility, namely this: the Kingdom was meant to be both spiritual and visible, internal and external; a Kingdom within the soul, and yet a Kingdom into which both soul and body have the power to come.

There remains the argument of futurity, as it may be called. Did Christ, in all that He said about the Kingdom of Heaven, intend to be understood as speaking of that perfected social state which is to ensue upon his coming again? In a word, did He mean the heavenly state itself, that which we look forward to when we pray, "Thy Kingdom come"?

Again let us resort to the parables. Two of the most familiar of them can settle this point in a moment. The Kingdom of Heaven, Jesus tells us, is like a net cast into the sea, that gathers of every kind, good and bad. And yet of the heavenly city of the future, that perfectly pure and holy city, we are told that there cannot enter into *it* anything that defileth, worketh abomination, or maketh a lie. In another place the Kingdom of Heaven is likened to a field of wheat in which an enemy sows tares. The wheat and tares grow together until the harvest. And when is the harvest? The harvest is "the end of the world." Clearly, then, the Kingdom of Heaven, as Christ uses the words, must be something that begins long before the world ends; otherwise how can it possibly be like a field in which wheat and tares grow together *until* the harvest?

The right way out of the difficulty seems to be this. When our Lord spoke of the Kingdom of Heaven, He had in mind a Kingdom He meant to establish at once here on earth, but a Kingdom, nevertheless, which should find its fullest and ripest development in the world to come. He was to lay the foundations in time, of a building whose battlements and spires were to mount up into eternity. If this was indeed his purpose, then it is certainly an unwise spirituality that allows itself to speak slightingly of organized Christianity as the "*mere* visible Church." Thus contemptuously to set aside the Church-Idea as being no part of the true Gospel of Christ, but only an accidental, perhaps dangerous appendage, is virtually to make ourselves wiser than our Lord Himself. Let us beware of endeavoring to be more spiritual than He whose gift the Spirit is.

We are sometimes warned of the great peril of putting the Church before Christ, or in the place of Christ. If by putting the Church before Christ be meant the worshipping of forms and ceremonies, instead of the worshipping of Almighty God, the caution is not amiss. But if it be meant that the Gospel of the Kingdom really interferes with or obscures the Gospel of the Cross, then the warning, however well meant, is a mistaken one. The New Testament couples together the two thoughts, "Christ" and "the Church." St. Paul agrees with this. He confesses that the mystery is great; "but," he adds, "I speak concerning Christ and the Church." St. John agrees with this. "The Spirit and the Bride say, Come." The Spirit is the Spirit of Christ; the Bride is the Church. In those high and mystic nuptials of which the Apostle speaks, the invisible and visible are wedded. What are we, that we should strive to have it otherwise? "Those whom God hath joined together, let no man put asunder."

Thus far we have been busy with determining the single point whether our Lord Jesus Christ did or did not mean that there should be built up in the world, after his departure, a visible and organized society bearing his name. Our next step will be to mark the manner in which the creative thought took shape and body in the hands of those who received it directly from the Founder.

We shall then review successively the three principal misapprehensions to which, in the progress of human history, the original thought has been subject, namely,—

    (a) Romanism, or the Exaggeration of the Divine
         Idea;

    (b) Puritanism, or the Diminution of the Divine
         Idea;

    (c) Liberalism, or the Distortion of the Divine
         Idea.

Lastly, we shall confront the difficult problem how in this strange new America of ours, good Christian people who sympathize fully with neither Romanism, Puritanism, nor Liberalism, but who desire to give each one of these its just due, may best be loyal to the true Church-Idea.

Let no one say that the inquiry is an idle one. Leastwise let no Christian man or woman say so.

For an unbeliever to boast, "The Church is nothing to me," is natural enough. But a believer has no right to use this flippant tone. In him indifference is blameworthy. He is as much bound to feel solicitude for the well-being of the Church, as the good citizen is bound to care for the prosperity of the State. For a Christian to declare that his whole religion consists in watering and weeding his own a spiritual garden-plot, and that he has no time to look beyond the hedge, is blank selfishness. We call the man who acknowledges no obligation to the community in which he lives a churl. The Church is the commonwealth of souls, and every Christian owes it fealty and service.

In following out the plan thus sketched, it will be the writer's aim to use perfectly explicit language so as to avoid being misunderstood. If at any time this plainness of speech should seem to the reader too plain, let him be assured that there is no intention of unkindness or discourtesy. The single purpose of these papers is to promote reconciliation and peace, a purpose which any least tinge of bitterness would thwart. But unity is to be sought through the truth; and if we would reach the truth everyman must say out honestly just what he thinks. When, therefore, in the course of our inquiry, different systems of religion are freely criticized it will be understood that this is due to no inability or unwillingness to appreciate what is good in them, but is only the fruit of an honest desire to get at the truth.

Any other method would be at once feeble and unsatisfactory. To say nothing directly, and to leave everything to inference, may be an inoffensive, as it certainly is a safe way of expressing thought. But what the most charitable of men has called "sound speech that cannot be condemned," is speech of another sort. It can only mean such utterance as is straightforward, intelligible, and to the point.

II. The Thought and Its Clothing

LIFE, of whatever sort it is, looks for a lodgment in organization. Perhaps the remark ought to be limited to life as we know it upon this planet. What the vital conditions may be elsewhere, we cannot tell. Here, certainly, life is forever taking on shapes that are at once its clothing and its expression.

Vegetable life finds its organization in roots and stalks, leaves and branches, plants and trees. Animal life breathes itself into flesh and bones, and seeks a dwelling in the bodies of all moving creatures, in birds, beasts, and men. There is yet a higher kind of life than either the vegetable or the animal. We call it spiritual life, the life that differences man from the brute.

Now where and how does this spiritual life find organization? In a partial and meager way the question is answered whenever spirit and flesh are welded together in one living man. But this embodiment is of necessity incomplete. It is the incarnation of *a* spirit, rather than of spirit. We must look for an ampler tabernacle than the human frame, and we find it in that large and complicated body, society. This is the law that binds men together in communities, girding the earth with a chain armor of families, each link nearly or distantly connected with every other link. The individual is conscious of incompleteness, and seeks instinctively, by joining himself to others of his kind, to realize that "fullness" which really can be gathered up in no one person save the Word made flesh. This, then, is the rationale of the Gospel of the Kingdom. This is the marrow of the Church-Idea. Because there has always been spiritual life in the world, *therefore* there has always been society. Because it is possible for the spirit of man to live either with God or apart from Him, *therefore* there has always been an inner or elect society—the Church. Because Jesus Christ brought into the world a vast access of spiritual life, *therefore* the new society of the elect in which this life has found embodiment is called, in distinction from the national election it displaced, the Catholic or Universal Church.

Now it is one thing to admit the truth of abstract statements like these, and quite another to discern their true bearing on the history of the past, and the needs of the present. We have undertaken to study the divine idea of the Church, but the attempt is hopeless without the aid of some sort of illustration.

Moreover, we want an illustration that shall carry with it the weight of authority. A man is at liberty to pick and choose illustrations when he is setting forth his own thoughts; but when he undertakes to interpret a revealed thought of God, we demand that he employ similitudes stamped with the sanction of the Revealer. Our Lord provided for this necessity very fully when He promulgated his Gospel of the Kingdom. He knew well that men would never catch his idea unless He put it into pictures, and wrote his own *Fecit* on the canvas. Both He and his Apostles after Him took pains, therefore, to employ very striking comparisons as a means of expounding the nature of the new society. Some of these comparisons illustrate one aspect of the divine idea, others another aspect.

Thus the Church is likened in the New Testament to a field of wheat, to a fisher's net, to a vineyard, to a kingdom, to a ship, to a sheepfold, to a family, to a bride, to a tree springing from a seed, to the human body. Of all these various similitudes, the last is richest in suggestion. Nothing in Nature is so marvelously wrought as the house that man inhabits, and it is no wonder we find it the best symbol of that Divine society whose Head is Christ, and whose many members are destined to constitute at last "the perfect man."

Besides, this illustration of the body falls in admirably with our present purpose, which is to ascertain in what way the Divine thought as it came from the mind of Christ took on, at the hands of his immediate successors, the clothing of actual fact. The

Apostle with whose activity in missionary labor we are best acquainted, was the same whose eye seems to have caught most readily the resemblance between the body and the Church. We are likely to find, therefore, that the analogy is as rich in practical suggestions as it is useful in the interpretation of ideal truth. Let us see.

The first and most obvious attribute of a body is Visibility. Undoubtedly there are bodies that we cannot see—microscopic bodies, for example, and ethereal bodies too subtle for our vision; but when we speak of such bodies as invisible, we really only mean that we have not the eyes to see them. Letting alone such fine-spun distinctions as this, the remark is perfectly true that the most obvious attribute of a body is visibility. It is, indeed, this very visibility that, in the common judgment of men, distinguishes body from spirit. Spirit is something that cannot be seen; body is something that can be seen. When the disciples after the resurrection were frightened because they thought they had seen a spirit, Jesus, while He reassured them, gently reproved their error of judgment. "Why are ye troubled? Behold my hands and my feet that it is I myself. Handle me and see, for a spirit hath not flesh and bones as ye see me have."[1] Here sight is made, by the highest authority, the criterion of the body's reality. "Handle me and *see.*" It is a true body, because it is a visible one.

If, then, the Church is a body, in any real and satisfactory sense, the Church must be a society that is visible, open to the eye. And what is a visible society? It is any union of men that confesses itself a union by having terms of admission and symbols of membership. The societies called "secret" are just as visible as any others, so far as the evidence of their existence goes. The nearest approach to an invisible society, if the very coupling of the two words does not involve a contradiction, is in the case of men banding together for the attainment of some object, and agreeing solemnly that their relation to each other shall not be indicated by any outward sign or token whatsoever. But we have a distinct name for such a union as this. We call it a conspiracy, or mingling of breaths. Yet even a breath upon a cold day takes form and shape such as the eye can see. So hard is it to disconnect the idea of visibility from the idea of a society.

Why, then, do we hear so much in these days about "the Church Invisible"? There certainly is no warrant for the phrase in Holy Scripture. Nowhere in the Word of God, from the first page of it to the last, is there any mention of a Church Invisible, save of that which is only invisible because it is in heaven, not on earth. We must remember that there is a difference between "things not seen" and things that cannot be seen. The heavenly Church is among the things not seen as yet, but this is not because it is a Church Invisible by nature. It can be seen, and will be seen, even as in vision it has been seen. Here is the picture of it. "After this I *beheld,* and lo, a great multitude which no man could number, of all nations, and kindreds, and people, and tongues, stood before the throne, and before the Lamb, clothed, with white robes, and palms in their hands; and cried with a loud voice, saying, Salvation to our God which sitteth upon the throne, and unto the Lamb."[2] This is indeed a Church to us invisible, and it is the only "Church Invisible" of which the Scriptures speak.

In the previous paper the argument against the theory of invisibility was rested upon the words of Christ Himself, and the question of his intention was made the central point. A glance at the actual practice of the men who were commissioned by Christ to carry out his plan will show whether the inference there drawn from the language of the King finds warrant in the acts of his lieutenants.

Let us see what was St. Paul's notion of edifying or building up that Body of Christ of which he said so much.

The Apostle goes into a certain city of Asia Minor, or Macedonia, or the Greek Peninsula, and he preaches there the Gospel of Jesus Christ. The soil is an outworn and unpromising one, but into it he bravely casts the seed. What follows? Some of the inhabitants of that city repent and believe. What follows next? The Apostle satisfies himself of the genuineness of their repentance and faith, and he then receives those persons and their households into the circle of the Kingdom, the Fold of the Church, the Body of Christ. How does he do this? He does it by that sacrament of Holy Baptism which the Lord Himself ordained as the door of entrance to the new society. They become regenerate, or new-born into the family of God.

The Apostle goes away. His missionary errand carries him to some far-off city of the Mediterranean. Presently he learns, either by some chance comer or by a special messenger, that all is not going on well in that city where he planted the Kingdom, and left it to be cared for at the hands of others. There has been a falling away from the faith, or dissensions have sprung up, or gross sins have crept in and defiled the flock, so that purity of life, as well as of faith, is put in peril. What does the Apostle now? He takes his pen, or he bids some fellow-missionary take the pen for him, and he writes a letter of counsel to those far-off Christians, telling them how sadly grieved he is to learn that anything has gone wrong, and pointing out in what way all may be set right again. But how does he address this letter? How should we expect him to address it, according to the "invisible Church" theory? Should we not look to find him drawing a sharp line of distinction at the very outset between those in the Church who had come up to his expectations, and those who had not? Should we not expect him to state explicitly that he regards those who have been in fault as no Christians at all? Ought he not to tell these last that their baptism was a nullity, that events have proved the sacrament to have been in their case an empty form, and bid them reflect that their membership of the mere "visible Church" avails them nothing?

This is what we might very naturally expect. But do we, in point of fact, find the Apostle taking this line? We know that the Christians of Corinth were, at one time, fallen into much such a state as has been pictured. St. Paul wrote to them. What was his address? "Paul, called to be an Apostle of Jesus Christ, through the will of God, and Sosthenes our brother, unto the Church of God which is at Corinth, to them that are sanctified in Christ Jesus, called to be saints, grace be unto you and peace."[3] The whole spirit of the letter is in harmony with this beginning. The Corinthian Christians, one and all, are dealt with throughout as those who had been sanctified, set apart to be holy, made members of the Body of Christ. The appeal to those of them who have gone astray is made to rest upon this very fact that they do belong, in virtue of their baptism, to the sacred Body of the Lord, and that they ought to be deeply penitent for having defiled that Body.

"As many of you as have been baptized into Christ have put on Christ;" this is the promise that underlies all his reasoning, the solemn reminder that gives weight to his every rebuke. Even when he is expostulating with the offenders themselves, his argument is that they are defiling the temple of God, "which temple," he significantly adds, "ye are." Does this look as if St. Paul had always in mind two Churches, an outer and an inner, a visible and an invisible, a husk and a kernel? Does it not rather look as if he regarded the whole body of the baptized as being the one Church of Christ on earth, a Church not without its unworthy and sickly members, even as the Lord had said should be, but still one Church, to be addressed as brethren, to be taught, to be guided, to be built up, to be ministered unto, to be led on in holy living, and, at last, to be judged, not by him, Paul, but by that One who is ordained to judge both them and him.

The mention just now made of the temple suggests a second point in the analogy between the Church and the living human body. What is it that gives honor to this complicated organism of flesh, and blood, and bones, and nerves, and muscles we call "the body"? It is the solemn fact that the body is the appointed dwelling place of a spirit. So long as it can claim this august tenant as its own, the body has dignity; but no sooner is the spirit fled from out it than the body begins to return into the crude and worthless elements of which it is built up. Beauty and power alike forsake it. Only dust remains.

Now what is it that makes the new society whose nature we are exploring worthy of the high and glorious titles given to it in Scripture? Doubtless it is the indwelling in this Body also of a Spirit. And what Spirit? God the Holy Ghost. Here lies the distinction between the Church and any other society whatsoever. The Church has the promise of its Divine Founder that He will be in it always.

And only consider what the presence of a spirit in a body involves. It is a most marvelous thing, this connection between ourselves and the temporary home in which we think and feel. The wit of man can formulate the law that keeps the stars in their courses, but of the law that links body to soul, it tells us almost nothing. We can philosophize upon that mysterious union, and invent all manner of hard names to describe it, but we get no nearer to understanding it by doing so. All that we really know about it is that it exists, and that it answers the purpose of making the body the servant and instrument of the soul. Thus, for example, you wish to express a thought in writing. Your will determines that your hand shall take the pen, dip it in ink, put it on the paper, form the words. But how did the mandate, which was a spiritual thing, find its way to the muscles of your hand? And, when it had reached them, how did it compel obedience? You answer, "By the power of volition." Yes, but are you any nearer to understanding *the thing,* because you have the phrase that describes it at your tongue's end? Not one whit.

And if we cannot understand how the spirit impels the body to action, neither do we know any better why it is that an injury done to the body brings grief and anguish to the spirit. By what strange electricity the nerves of feeling are empowered to carry to the soul their nimble messages of warning, and, as it were, bring down the spirit to the suffering part, who can comprehend? We only know that thus it is. The ancients used to say, The soul is all in every part. We moderns have not got beyond the paradox.

It is impossible to appreciate the wealth of St. Paul's illustration unless we take into account this omnipresence of the spirit in the body. Let the reader summon up to his mind the image of a vast society of living men, all animated, actuated, and controlled by one central spirit. Let him imagine that spirit sending out commands to every remotest point of the complex organism, just as a human will telegraphs its orders to hand or foot, to eye or lip. Let him imagine again that spirit receiving intelligence from all these various members, learning of their necessities, knowing when they suffer, sorrowing, as it were, with their sorrow, rejoicing in their joy. "Now the Lord is that Spirit": His body is the Church. His going forth upon the nerves of motion we call "grace." Our coming to Him upon the return nerves of feeling we call "prayer." What a marvelous similitude it is! How can we enough adore the wisdom that has thus made the seen things the mirror of the unseen; our perishable and earthly frame the type of that Body Mystical which is the dwelling place of Christ!

A third important point in this analogy is that which bears upon the question of the Church's unity. That the Church ought to be visibly, as well as spiritually one, is a direct corollary from the two truths already brought out. It is wonderful that even the usages of common speech do not teach people to see more clearly the connection between life and unity. Thus, for instance, while a man is living, we say that he is one person, but after he is dead, we speak of his "remains." Why this change of number from the singular to the plural? It is because a body, taken by itself, suggests manifoldness of parts; and when the tenant whose presence brought all things into unity has fled, the characteristic which was before subordinate, becomes conspicuous. Similarly we make "dissolution" a synonym of death; and what is dissolution but a sundering into parts of that which before was whole? Are those who maintain that the competition of sects makes the life of the Church aware that what they advocate is really nothing less than the dissolution of the Body of Christ? Indeed, is it not something worse than dissolution? The demoniac who had Legion for his guest would probably have chosen death as a relief; and yet the only way by which sectarianism can escape the charge of crucifying the Lord afresh is by taking refuge in the idea of a Body multitudinously possessed. An alternative more awful it would be hard to name.

We are assured that there must be "diversities of operation," and hence sects. By all means let us admit the first proposition; by no means let us consent to the inference. Diversity is perfectly consistent with oneness; sectarianism not at all. Nature is running over with variety, but it is a variety in unity, a diversity that is absolutely obedient to law.

That the modern interpretation of the phrase just quoted would have been wholly alien to the mind of its author is evident from the peremptory way in which we find him dealing with the sectarian principle in his own times. He does not seem to have regarded the Cephas party and the Apollos party as harmless "diversities of operation," in which the Corinthian Church might safely be indulged. On the contrary he did not hesitate to say that such divisions savored more of worldliness than of godliness. No, this theory that the eye of the Almighty discerns in sectarian Christianity a harmony hidden from man's weaker vision is but a poor makeshift at best. The definition of unity that it implies is such a definition as would not be admitted for a moment in connection with any of those forms of community-life most familiar to us. Who, for instance, would dream of organizing a commonwealth, a university, an army, or a navy, upon this principle that outward and visible unity need not be considered as particularly important? And if the higher we rise in the development of social life, the more we feel the need of a perfect order, why should we imagine that in the structure of the ideal community, the Church, this point may be safely disregarded?

But these are questions that properly belong to a later stage of our inquiry. At present they are only noted in their connection with the argument from analogy. If the Church be a living body, unity belongs to it of right.

One more resemblance: In every human body that lives and breathes there goes forward a process of ceaseless change. The vital energies are constantly engaged in discarding old material, and assimilating new. The atoms of carbon, hydrogen, oxygen, and nitrogen that have done their work go on their way to build up other bodies, and fresh atoms come in to take their place. Physiologists have not decided what precise period of time is required for an entire change of fleshly clothing; but that such a change does take place many times over in the course of an ordinary life they are agreed. The identity of a man's body is, therefore, something quite different from that of a marble statue,[4] for it is an identity that must, somehow, be consistent with perpetual change. Now and then there come crises in the history of a body. We call them diseases. They may leave the man in a better condition than they found him, or they may leave him in a worse. They may alter his outward appearance for the remainder of his life, or, again, they may alter it only temporarily. In either case, and in any case, a man's body, so long as he inhabits it, remains his body still.

The bearing of these facts upon the phenomena of Church life is important. We talk about Reformations of the Church, and argue whether they are desirable or not. Reformations? Why, the whole life of the Church ought to be a continual Reformation, a constant taking out of the way that which is effete, and re-forming the tissue with new material. Those who fancy that in order to demonstrate the identity of the Church they must import into the nineteenth century the cultus of the thirteenth are under a delusion. As well refuse to own your friend because his countenance at forty is not what it was at twenty-five, as turn suspicious of the Church of your fathers because it does not look to you precisely as it looked to them. Provided the historical continuity of the Church be kept, and the original deposit of faith preserved intact, it matters not how many reformations are experienced. An unintermitting reformation would be the best of all. Thus we gather from this analogy of the Body no less than four notes, or characteristics of the perfect Church:

1. Visibility.
2. The indwelling Spirit of the Lord.
3. Unity.
4. Capability of perpetual renewal.

But how has it fared with this Divine idea in the actual history of the world? This is a question upon which we have yet to enter. We must approach it prepared for some measure of disappointment, and even of mortification.

Every one is familiar with the distinction between an idea and its realization. A man conceives some grand and noble thought, and he attempts to give expression to it, but he invariably fails. What we call works of art are but the forms or shapes into which men have cast their various thoughts and imaginings. The one word written upon them all is Imperfection.

No matter what the work is, be it a picture, a poem, a statue, a building, a machine, an oratorio, the maker of it will be the first to acknowledge, if he be an artist indeed, that that which seems so perfect in the eyes of others, does, in his own, fall short of what he can imagine. Between a high idea and man's embodiment of it there is always a great gulf fixed.

It is told of the famous Danish sculptor, that in later life he was once found in his studio laboring under deep dejection. He gave it as the cause of his melancholy that he had just completed a work that satisfied him. "My powers must be on the decline," he added, "when I find that I am contented with anything that I accomplish." This must always be the confession of honest human endeavor. Our best achievements lag behind our visions of what might be.

The history of the Church of Christ is but the record of a long and painful effort to clothe in actual fact the divine idea of a heavenly kingdom upon earth. But in this, as in all else with which man has to do, the result has been lamentably imperfect.

Is it objected that such an admission is inconsistent with what has been said about the divine origin of the Church-Idea? Not at all. The divine thought, it is true, must be perfect for the very reason that it is divine. But the working out of the thought has been left, to a great degree, in the hands of men. Part of the purpose was that in this building of the Temple we should be "laborers together with God." God's share in the work has indeed been perfect; ours very far from perfect. This is why it was said that we should find cause for mortification; for is anything more mortifying, when we have the picture of what might be, and of what was meant to be, before our eyes, than to observe in what a sad and terrible way human willfulness, and human pride, and human enmity have marred and disfigured in the fulfillment the fair beauty of the promise?

And yet, along with our mortification, we shall feel gratitude and joy, if we discover that, after all, the lines of the original painting are still traceable upon the stained and torn canvas, and that underneath the incrustations of long ages there lies the pure and perfect outline of the Mystical Body of the Lord.

III. Romanism:
The Idea Exaggerated

IN one of his latest addresses to the pilgrim Israelites, Moses made a point of warning them against the temptation to tamper with the Law they had received. "Ye shall not add," he said, "unto the word that I command you, neither shall ye diminish aught from it." The people understood that their Leader claimed this perfectness for his Law solely on the ground of its having come from God. Their acquiescence was but a confession of the general truth that God's handiwork cannot be bettered by man's skill. Thus the precept covered a principle, and a principle which is as true now as it was then. A Revelation once given is susceptible to improvement at no hand save the Revealer's. We may use our ingenuity in interpreting and applying its contents; but until it has been superseded by a new revelation of paramount authority, our simple duty is to guard it alike from increment and loss.

In the course of our inquiry into the true nature of the Church of Christ, we have reached a point where the application of this principle is of the utmost importance. The adherents of the religious system known as Romanism claim for themselves that they, and they alone of living men, are in communion with the true Body Mystical of our Lord Jesus Christ. In their view, the Papal Church is the Catholic Church; and if the Catholic Church, then the Church of the Apostles; and if the Church of the Apostles, then the Church of Christ; and if the Church of Christ, then the City of God, the Kingdom of Heaven upon earth, the Mother of us all.

Grant the first proposition, and the rest follow. But is the first proposition true? Do the cause of the Papacy and the cause of Catholicity indeed stand and fall together? Certainly not, if it can be shown that Rome has overlaid with inventions of her own the original constitution of the Kingdom—has so blotted the charter of our rights that it is hard for the unskilled eye to read the words as they were written.

But first let it be frankly admitted that there is a great deal to give color to the claims of Rome both in the line of reasoning and of observation. Starting from the "*Tu es Petrus*" as her historical premise, and from Christ's assurance that the Paraclete should guide the Church into all truth as her theological premise, Rome weaves her argument for authority out of a warp of realism and a woof of idealism. It is an argument not to be despised, and those who hold a different view of

Catholicity are bound to show how Rome's claims are to be met.

The late Archbishop Whately is said to have once posed a whole tableful of his clergy by taking up the defense of Romanism, and calling on his guests to furnish counter-arguments. They were finally compelled to beseech him that he would confute himself. The spectacle must have been as pitiable as it was ludicrous. The men ought to have been, as no doubt they were, heartily ashamed of themselves. Had Archer Butler been at the dinner, at least one Irish churchman would have held his own against the Primate.

The helplessness of Protestant apologists is often due to their having taken up an entirely false and mistaken line of defense. There are two ways of dealing with this question of Romanism: one is the method of denunciation, the other that of calm inquiry and impartial search. Everybody knows that the first is the more usual method. It is so for the simple reason that denunciation is always easier, and sometimes more effective, than argument. A zealous Protestant can quickly gather an armful of epithets from Daniel and the Apocalypse, and shower them without mercy upon the whole Roman Communion. Thus we often hear the Pope unhesitatingly called Antichrist or the Man of Sin. The learning of Roman Catholic theologians and the piety of Roman Catholic devotees are spoken of with similar contempt. The one is represented to be the mere offspring of credulity; the other, if it be not hypocrisy, is plainly the base lust of reward. Whatever looks like goodness in a Romanist is, we are assured, nothing more than a spurious imitation of the reality. No holiness is genuine that is not also Protestant. This method of combating the errors of Romanism may perhaps be justified by the law of retaliation, for Rome herself has not been sparing of her curses, but it certainly cannot be justified by the law of love. As disciples of Him who bade his followers bless and curse not, let us aim at the more excellent way. A sentence to carry weight need not be rounded with an anathema, nor can a weak argument ever be buttressed with hard words.

Besides, there is a special reason why the popular war-cries of "intolerance," "bigotry," "priestcraft," "ambition," and the like should be avoided. These wholesale charges are as dangerous as they are vague; double-edged swords, they may be made to cut both ways. No doubt Romanism, in the day of her power, was fiercely intolerant. But has Protestantism, in her day, never been intolerant? We need not go beyond the limits of New England for an answer. The truth is, majorities are almost always intolerant. Romanists, in this matter, are only like other men. When they are weak, they advocate tolerance. When they are strong, they are tempted to intolerance. And so with the other charges of bigotry, priestcraft, and ambition. If individual Romanists are bigoted, crafty, and ambitious, so are also individual Protestants the same. And if individual Protestants are large-hearted, honest, and of lowly mind, so are also individual Romanists the same.

You draw your dark picture of the bigot, of Alva, of Loyola, of Pole. The Romanist confronts you with Fénelon, with Pascal, with Montalembert. You hold up some perfidious Jesuit to contempt. The Romanist reminds you of those heroic missionaries who were among the first martyrs to Christ here in our own America. You talk about ambition. Your adversary points to the divisions among Protestants, and asks tauntingly, Who are the more ambitious, they who are ready to sacrifice their personal preferences to the common welfare, or they who will rend the sacred Body of Christ rather than not see their own pet scheme triumphant?

It is probably true that the tendency of Romanism, as a system, is to beget and foster intolerance, bigotry, priestcraft, and ambition. The writer does not dispute the point; but he declines, in an inquiry like this, to press these charges, for the simple reason that they are such as may be bandied to and fro forever. For the purposes of argument they are vague and inconclusive as compared with the more important accusation to which we are about to turn. Passing them all by, therefore, let us rest the argument against Rome upon the simple fact that she has added to the faith. This is the one charge from which that Church has never cleared herself, the weighty charge of having imposed upon the flock of Christ both usages and doctrines of which the Chief Shepherd never knew. That she has been untrue to the pure Gospel that was of old entrusted to the faithful, is her crime.

But how are we to ascertain what this pure Gospel was? That it had an existence is very certain. Evidently, to the Apostles' thinking, there could be no greater treason against Christ than to supplement or alter the sacred deposit left in the keeping of, the Church, "the faith once delivered to the saints."

The only trustworthy information we possess with regard to this original deposit comes from the Christian Scriptures. Apart from all arguments about inspiration, it is indisputable that these writings furnish the sole authentic record of what Jesus Christ Himself said and taught, and what the men who were under his immediate guidance said and taught after Him. Of course the oral teaching of the Apostles preceded their written instructions, and it is here that Rome brings in her plea for tradition. But the best tradition can scarcely be compared in value with documentary evidence; and when they are satisfied that they have the latter, men care little for the former. Only in so far as the oral teaching of the founders of the Church is embodied in the book called the New Testament, do we know with any certainty what it was.

Hence it was that the Church of the Anglo-Saxon race planted herself, in the great awakening of the sixteenth century, upon this broad and settled principle that Holy Scripture is the only perfectly trustworthy depository of revealed truth. Here is her authoritative

language: "Holy Scripture containeth all things necessary to salvation; so that whatsoever is not read
therein, nor may be proved thereby, is not to be
required of any man that it should be believed as an
article of the faith, or be thought requisite or necessary to salvation."[2] The language with regard to the
primitive creeds is in harmony with this. They are
received upon the express ground that their statements "may be proved by most certain warrants of
Holy Scripture."[3]

Here we touch the heart of the question. Rome is
arraigned upon the charge of having imposed upon
the faithful, as essential to salvation, articles of belief
that cannot possibly be proved by Holy Scripture. Is
this charge true? There is a distinction drawn by
Roman theologians between what they call "pious
opinions" and the actual articles of the faith. Readers
of recent controversy have been made very familiar
with this distinction; but others may ask for an expla-
nation. A "pious opinion," then, is a belief that may be
very generally entertained among the faithful, while
yet it lacks the official seal of the Church's authority.
Such an opinion may, at a given time, be exerting far
more influence over the minds and hearts of the people than anyone of the accredited articles of faith, but
so long as it is not defined as dogma, it is an "opinion"
still; it may be reckoned a virtue to receive it, but it is
not counted a sin to doubt it, nor a mortal sin to reject
it. Many of the superstitious notions for which the
Roman Church is popularly held accountable, really

belong to the class of pious opinions. No skilled con-
fessor would ever allow an educated Protestant to
make these a barrier to his conversion. Nothing is easier than to see in them merely the moss and ivy that
soften the outline of an ancient minster wall.

If the additions Rome has made to the pure faith
of the Church were nothing more than "pious opinions," the law of Christian charity would perhaps
demand that we should look upon them indulgently,
and not regard them as an insuperable bar to peace.
But those additions of which most serious complaint
is made are not held by Rome as "pious opinions,"
they are taught as dogma, and have the full sanction
of that Church's authority. Our own times have wit-
nessed the actual transformation by a Papal mandate
of what was, twenty years ago, a "pious opinion," into
an article of the faith, essential to salvation.[4]

In the year 1849 Pius IX wrote to the Bishops of
the Roman communion throughout the world, asking
them severally whether in their judgment the right
time had come to define as dogma the "pious opinion" that the Blessed Virgin Mary was conceived without stain of original sin. To this circular very many of
the most learned and devout among the Bishops
replied in the language of respectful remonstrance.
Some did not reply at all. The answers returned were
collected and printed, and the copious extracts from
them given in a note to Dr. Pusey's "Eirenicon"[5] make
the most interesting feature of that learned work.

The reserved and guarded style of many of the communications is very curious. It is a significant fact that of the twenty-eight Roman Bishops then resident in the United States, only one, and he the occupant of a comparatively unimportant see, sent any answer at all. Of the Bishops and Archbishops of France, only a bare majority expressed themselves in favor of promulgating the proposed decree. A large number of the German Bishops advised against it. But the almost perfect unanimity of the Italian, Spanish, and Irish ecclesiastics carried the day, and in the year 1854 a decree went forth from the Papal chair authoritatively assigning to the human mother of our Lord an attribute which Holy Scripture gives only to Jesus Christ Himself.[6]

We are the more struck by the boldness, some would say the effrontery of this deliberate addition to the faith of the Church for the reason that it has taken place so recently; but in reality we ought to be equally sensitive to all violations of the principle that a revelation cannot be mended by man's wit. An English theologian has depicted in a most striking way the gradual process by which, through neglect of this principle, modern error has become mixed up with primitive truth. The illustration is so perfect that no apology need be made for quoting it at length.

"Let the whole body of dogmatic truth" (and by this expression is meant all that is authoritatively taught as *de fide* by any recognized body of Christians) "be considered together. Whatever we may think of the doctrine, let us view the whole as one stream; then let us trace it backward to its fountainhead, and see what happens. The process is the same as tracing a river to its source. We wish to know whence it derives its waters; we therefore trace it carefully up the stream, and note where every branch separates, to the right hand, or to the left. No stream that falls in anywhere along the course can form any part of the original waters; we therefore let it alone, and steadily pursue the central current, till we reach the spot where it flows out of the broad lake or the precipitous mountain-side.

"Let us do the same thing with the dogmatic teaching of the Church; we shall then see which branch traces its origin furthest back, and forms part of the parent stream. We scarcely commence the process before one doctrine is separated from the mass and falls behind us. The dogma of the immaculate conception of the Virgin Mary reaches no farther back than our own memories. Steadily tracing the course of time backwards, the dogma of purgatorial fire branches off about the middle of the sixteenth century, and dies away as a formal doctrine about the middle of the twelfth. In the early part of the fifteenth century the mutilation of the sacrament of the Lord's Supper, by taking away the cup from the laity, disappears. A little further back, at the beginning of the thirteenth century, we find transubstantiation for the first time dogmatically taught, and in another two or three centuries all traces of it are lost again. In the twelfth century five of the seven sacraments disappear, and the two 'ordained by Christ Himself' alone survive. In the ninth century the power of canonization for the first time falls into the stream of doctrine, although tendency to saint worship and to incipient Mariolatry reaches further backward. In the beginning of the sixth century the papal supremacy is left behind, and with it the last formal trace of the corrupt dogmas of the East and West."

He then follows back the undivided stream of truth until he comes to the first century. Here he pauses. Somehow, in that mysterious century, the river had its earthly birth. "Here, for an historical certainty, the faith begins. This admits of no denial....We stand, as it were, looking into the depths mysterious, yawning beneath and before the eye, inscrutable and unfathomable, whence the waters spring into the daylight. Look and watch and wonder. What spring is capacious enough to have given them birth? The channel itself we can see to be as human as ourselves, though of finer and purer soil, as if the ever-gushing fountains of truth close by had clothed it with perennial beauty and verdure. Whence it issues the outward eye cannot see. The spring is there where no human hand can reach, no human foot can tread. It lies in the unseen, not the seen. Stand and watch the waters. All the dear familiar truths are there known to us from our childhood, almost the very words in which the Church is accustomed to express them. How sweetly, purely, freshly, vigorously they well forth from the fountain infinite, for that fount is GOD."[7]

In this singularly lucid figure, we have the argument against Rome stated with tremendous power. For this is what we charge upon her, that she has suffered to flow into the pure stream of God's truth tributaries that have defiled it. She has added to the word that Christ commanded. She has exaggerated the Divine idea.[8]

A few words as to the present aspects of Romanism in this country. Nowhere in the world, perhaps, does the Papal religion appear to so great advantage as here. Nowhere are its adherents more justly confident of the future. The repulsive features of the system, that meet one at every turn in countries where it has been long established, are among us so toned down and modified that its best points are also its salient points. The devotion of the people to their religion; their willingness to make the heaviest personal sacrifice for its maintenance and advancement; their universal recognition of the positive duty of worship; these are telling arguments with men who make earnestness the only sure test of sincerity. It is simple justice to the Romanists of America to acknowledge that in these points they set an example that ought to put Protestantism to the blush.

Making all due allowance for the secondary motives that may have fanned their zeal, there yet remains a large amount of single-hearted devotion and self-sacrifice that we cannot discredit without falling into the sin of calling good evil, and evil good. For all this they have their reward. The fact that their Church has been, thus far, the Church of the poor and the unlettered, so far from being against them, will in the end inure to their advantage. The Church of Christ began by being the Church of the poor, and never is she stronger than when she is willing to continue the Church of the poor.

American Romanists have their reward also in this, that their devoted attachment to their religion has had the effect of drawing the attention of thinking men to the historical and philosophical aspects of their system. The mistake of Protestants in this country has been, all along, the common one of undervaluing the resources and abilities of their adversary. Our religious writers and platform orators have suffered themselves (probably out of ignorance) to speak with the utmost scorn of the intellectual claims of Romanism. Looking only at the patent fact that the bulk of Roman Catholics in this country are rude, uncultivated people, they have drawn the hasty inference that the Roman Catholic religion can only be honestly received by such as are rude and uncultivated, and they have declaimed accordingly.

Such a view of the subject is only the result of a narrowed horizon. The truth is that Roman Catholicism has its intellectual as well as its popular side, and that, in some of its aspects, it appeals even more strongly to the educated than to the uneducated mind.

Whatever influence the grandeur of historical associations can exert, whatever power of persuasion logical subtlety can carry with it, whatever enchantment poetry and art can weave around the aesthetic faculties of the soul, these Rome has at her disposal, and will use when the occasion calls.

Our people are just becoming aware of the existence of this side of the subject. It is a surprise to them, and one result of the surprise will be that many will pass from an undue contempt for the Church of Rome into an undue admiration of her.

Very few deliberately embrace Romanism at present, unless from honest conviction. But, as time goes on, we shall probably see a marked change in this respect. We Americans have a constitutional bias towards the idolatry of success. When any enterprise succeeds, no matter how we may have hated it or opposed it in its progress, we are tempted to fall down and worship it simply because it has succeeded.

Rome, with her increasing advantages, will, in the future, be very likely to secure the adhesion of that large class which sways to and fro, backwards and forwards, agreeably to the alternations of success.

But let us remember that although lapse of time and change of fashions may make error respectable, they never can make error true.

Even should Rome attain, during the coming generation, to that ascendancy in America for which she so patiently labors, and after which she so fervently aspires, an ascendancy than which only one other is more to be deprecated, even then Rome would be no more right than she is right today. If she has indeed added, and added falsely, to the simple Gospel of the Kingdom, such additions will not be lessened, nor made innocent by the flight of years.

No "theory of development,"[9] skillfully wrought as it may be, can ever prove the mistletoe to have been in the acorn around the offspring of whose womb it clings. Like produces and develops like, and there are features of Romanism for the like of which we search the New Testament in vain. Let this nation heed well the Apostolic warning, "Stand fast therefore in the liberty wherewith Christ hath made us free, and be not entangled again in the yoke of bondage"—a yoke that history tells us our fathers found themselves not able to bear, and which it would be a sad folly in us their sons voluntarily to assume.

IV. Puritanism:
The Idea Diminished

IF a handful of steel dust be mixed with a dozen handfuls of sand, and then a magnet drawn hither and thither through the heap, the fine metallic particles, yielding to the mysterious law of their nature, are drawn away, while the dull, unsusceptible, passionless grains of flint remain. Following the old Hebrew usage of enforcing a spiritual truth by some outward parabolic act, one might make this simple experiment a symbol of what is known as the Puritan theory of religion. Suppose the mingled heap to represent the human race. Forget the truth that this same race is a family knit together by its myriad bands of kinship, and look upon it only as a vast congeries of individuals. Of these individuals a certain definite number are salvable, and the Gospel is the magnet by which they are to be reached. The children of light feel the attraction of the cross. Upon the children of darkness it has no power save to condemn. There ensues a process of separation, and those who are thus singled out from the gross body of their fellow men constitute the Church of the Redeemed.

In characterizing this view of Christianity as "the Puritan theory," the writer intends no disrespect to a word which many excellent and godly people hold in high esteem. Some words force themselves upon us by their very perspicuity. "Puritan" and "Puritanism" define with wonderful exactness the reality that lies behind them, and to this felicity of structure they owe their present use. The root of these significant words is *pure*. The Puritan is he who proposes to cleanse or make *pure* the Church of Christ by narrowing it to the circle of those of whose acceptance with the Almighty there is perfectly satisfactory proof. Looking constantly in imagination upon the picture of the Church triumphant, that "glorious Church, not having spot, or wrinkle, or any such thing," the Puritan is impatient and dissatisfied because the actual Kingdom corresponds so poorly with the ideal. He is convinced that the fault must be wholly in the line of administration, in the management of the power of the keys. He urges continually a more faithful discipline, and counts it little short of an impiety to call the Church the "Body of the Lord" so long as there is to be seen upon its surface any spot or stain. He loves better to dwell upon the thought of the "few chosen" than upon the thought of the "many called." The "little flock" means more to him than the "ten thousand times ten thousand, and thousands of thousands." Naturally to the Puritan the external unity of the Church appears a thing of small moment as compared with its internal sanctity. Better, he argues, separation than corruption. Let us make sure of purity even though we jeopard peace. Let us be continually cleansing the Kingdom, even at the risk of turning it upside down.

That this view of the nature of the Church of Christ has its true side, it would be useless to deny. A theory which has found so many zealous and able advocates cannot be wholly wrong. The most careless reader of the Scriptures must have noticed how much prominence is given in them to the ideas of election and separation, the two points upon which the parable of the magnet turns. As the inquiry proceeds full credit will be given to these elements of truth, and their harmony with the principles of genuine Catholicity made plain.

But it is one thing to admit that a system has truth in it, and quite another to declare that system true. The Puritan is undoubtedly right in demanding that the Church's standard of holiness shall be kept at the highest mark. He is undoubtedly wrong when he makes admission to the Fold, or continuance in it, dependent upon the individual's near approach to this. The Church's standard is one of aspiration, not attainment. Content with nothing short of perfection, she yet, like her divine Head, bears with imperfection. Let the harvest be gathered now, she says, and winnowed at the Judgment Day. Thus it appears that the issue is between the two ideas of inclusiveness and exclusiveness, comprehension and selection.

On the one side stands the Puritan demanding that the books be opened and the sentence given at once; against him are the Words of Jesus, the Practice of the Apostles, the Experience of History.

I. The Words of Jesus

"The kingdom of heaven is like unto a net, that was cast into the sea, and gathered of every kind: which when it was full they drew to shore, and sat down, and gathered the good into vessels, but cast the bad away. So shall it be at the end of the world." Had Christ said nothing else about the nature of his Church, this in itself would, be decisive. The parable cannot possibly be interpreted of the Kingdom of Heaven that is within us, for there is an evident distinction made in it between individuals good and bad. It cannot possibly be interpreted of the Kingdom of Heaven that is to come when the kingdoms of this world shall have passed away, for then how should we explain the reference to the Judgment? There is but one straightforward and honest way of dealing with the words, and that is to apply them to the Church on earth. Christ means to teach us that in his present Kingdom there must of necessity be a mingling of the holy and the unholy, the worthy and the worthless. When the net is full, the good are to be severed from the bad. When the election is complete, the selection is to begin.

The College of the Apostles, which was the embryo Church, had from the beginning this mingled character. The Son of Man knew what was in man, and yet of the twelve whom He called to Himself to be his especial bodyguard, one was a pronounced traitor, another sacrificed fealty to fear, another said, "Except I shall see in his hands the print of the nails, I will not believe." Treachery, timidity, and doubt all had their representatives even in that little band to whom the King entrusted the fortunes of his realm.

It would seem, then, that in so far as we can know the mind of Christ by observing what He said and what He did, we are bound to believe that He intended his Church to rest upon the inclusive and comprehensive principle rather than the opposite. If this be so, there is not only no unfairness, there is great propriety in defining Puritanism as a Diminution of the Divine Idea. Rome adds a cubit to the stature of the body mystical of Christ, and thus hurts it by excess. But it is quite as possible to mar that faultless form by belittling its majesty. The "perfect man" to whom St. Paul likens the united and developed Church is neither a giant nor a dwarf. Addition and subtraction are alike fatal to the Gospel's symmetry. The one error gives us grossness; the other, insignificance.

II. The Practice of the Apostles

During the forty days that intervened between our Lord's rising from the dead and his Ascension, the disciples, we are told, received from Him instruction in

"the things pertaining to the kingdom of God." Our
only means of ascertaining the purport of that mysterious tuition, is to observe in what way the Apostles
went to work, after they had received it. The signal
value of the Book of Acts lies in the fact that there we
find recorded this very thing, namely, what the Apostles *did*. Thus it would seem that this second branch
of our inquiry is really but another form of the first.
We are still looking to the words of Jesus for our
authority, only we read them as translated into actual
fact by the hands of those to whom they were committed. In brief, granting that our Lord gave to his
infant kingdom a definite charter or constitution, there
can be no safer guide to the interpretation of it than
Apostolic practice.

The question, then, is this: Did the Apostles
administer the Church upon the Puritan principle, or
did they not?

Undoubtedly in so far as Puritanism is synony-
mous with unusual strictness of life and simplicity of
manners, the Twelve were Puritans. The image of holiness they held up was without fleck or blemish. They
desired the Church to mirror this image in its perfectness. But did they seek the fruition of their hope
by enforcing an exclusive regimen? Recall the familiar story of their ministry. No sooner had they
received the promised gift of guidance than they went
out into all lands, proclaiming, as ambassadors of
God, forgiveness to a waiting world. The story of the
cross and the story of the Resurrection made the sta-

ple of their message. They preached "a death unto sin," because Christ had died, the just for the unjust. They preached "a new birth unto righteousness," because Christ had risen, and opened unto men the gate of everlasting life.

It was a simple Gospel, very simple indeed. Among the people who listened to them, many repented and believed. These, after due instruction, the ambassadors received into the kingdom by a sacramental rite, and from that time forth they were addressed and treated as heirs of the promises, as children adopted into the family of God, as members of the mystical Body of the Lord Jesus Christ. If afterwards some among these converted persons showed signs of weakness, whether in matter of faith or life; if they yielded to this or that temptation, and in the heat of the conflict with the Evil One gave way once and again, the chief pastors did not call upon the Church to cast out the offending brother that the Body might be kept pure; but they bade the community use kindness and forbearance, that the erring one might be brought back, the fallen lifted up and made to stand.

Not that there was no discipline exercised in the Primitive Church. On the contrary, this branch of church government was probably in a more healthy condition under the immediate eye of the Apostles than it ever has been since. We know that in one particular instance St. Paul resorted to the extreme measure of excommunication. No doubt it was the unanimous teaching of the Apostolic Company that the hopelessly bad, the manifestly irreclaimable members should be cut off from the communion of the faithful. And yet in reading the Book of Acts and the Epistles, it is difficult to say which strikes us more forcibly, the earnestness of the exhortations to holiness, or the evident willingness to deal charitably and patiently with those members of the community who fail to reach the standard of what a Christian ought to be.

How often St. Paul, for instance, put in a word for "the weak brethren"! How constantly he urges kindness, forbearance, pity, as motives that ought especially to guide the stronger members of the flock. We do not find in his words the faintest trace of any sentimental, feeble indulgence towards sin; but we do find the most generous and large-hearted spirit of love towards the sinning man or woman who needs to be called back and helped. The Church, as the Apostles present it, is a training school into which all are to be received who honestly desire to come. The Master of this school is Christ. They themselves are but ministers, or under-teachers, entrusted with the practical details of management, but in all things subject to the supreme will of the Head. In this school the very highest standard of attainment is to be constantly held up in both the departments of character and scholarship, but at the same time a wise patience must be exercised with those who fail to reach the standard, and even the risk of retaining some unworthy member is to be incurred rather than that any be too hastily excluded.

The illustration is an imperfect one, as any human illustration of a many-sided divine truth must be. It is imperfect because the Church is something more than a school of learners or disciples; it is a company of redeemed souls, pardoned mortals received back to the forfeited privilege of communion with their Maker. But the illustration, albeit inadequate, serves well enough to bring out the important point, namely, that according to the original plan the Christian Church was meant to be an inclusive, comprehensive, catholic society, and not the opposite. Any system, therefore, that proposes to curtail, narrow, or diminish the largeness of the blessing thus bestowed upon the world does violence to the purpose of our Lord.

III. The Experience of History

How has Puritanism succeeded as a practical working system? The principle has repeatedly asserted itself in the history of Christianity. Has it borne sweet fruit or bitter? It might seem natural in making this appeal, to consider first of all the case of English Puritanism as being that embodiment of the separatist theory most familiar to the general reader. But it will be well to avoid doing this, for the reason that so many political and quasi-political questions are mixed up with the history of English Puritanism as to make the use of it as an illustration perilous. It is above all things desirable, in such an inquiry as this, to avoid anything that may stir prejudice, or put an artificial bias on the judgment. It so happens that we can find a very satisfactory instance of the conflict in actual experience between the two theories of the Church, the exclusive and the inclusive, so ancient as even to antedate that union between Church and State which gives to the question of Puritanism in England and America its complicated character.

In the early ages of Christianity, before the faith of the cross had become one of the "tolerated religions" of the Roman Empire, there arose from time to time hot persecutions. When these fever-fits of pagan hate came on, a tremendous pressure was brought to bear upon all who were unwilling to deny the faith. The tests of renunciation demanded by the civil authorities differed in the different persecutions. At one time the plan was to compel the Christians to abjure their religion by giving them the alternative of burning incense to the heathen gods or suffering torture. At another time an emperor conceived the idea of exterminating the hated sect by causing the destruction of all the sacred books of the Christians, the precious records of the faith.

As might have been anticipated, there were among the brethren different degrees of resistance to these attempts. Loyalty to Christ ranged all the way from the unflinching constancy of the martyrs, who surrendered life itself rather than waver in their allegiance, down to the timid time-serving of those who at the first note of alarm hastened to give in their

adhesion to the religion of the state. Those who suc-
cumbed under the influence brought to bear upon
them were classified by their fellow Christians according to the degree of their inconstancy. There were
some, for instance, who secured indemnity from persecution by purchasing from the magistrates certifi-
cates to the effect that they had sacrificed to the
heathen gods, although in point of fact they had not
done so. This was reckoned a milder and more venial
form of apostasy than theirs who voluntarily went over
to the pagan side. Then there were "the traditors," as
those were called who surrendered their copies of the
Holy Scriptures, whence our word "traitor." There
were also "the sacrificers" and "the incense-burners,"
names significant of the particular act by which the
faith had been betrayed.

Now when there came a lull, a longer or shorter
period of quiet after a persecution, the question naturally arose in the Church, How should those whose
timidity had overmastered their loyalty be treated?
Should "the lapsed," as the whole body of the unfaith-
ful were called, be received back into church-fellow-
ship, or should the gates of the City of God be closed
on them forever?

Opinions were divided. On the one side there was
the desire to vindicate the purity of the Church, and
an unwillingness to seem to make light of the heinous
sin of denying Christ. On the other side there was the
memory of Peter's denial and his Lord's forgiveness

of him, together with a reluctance to drive into despair those who seemed to be deeply penitent for their weakness and terribly ashamed of it. The milder party were in favor of receiving back the weak brethren after satisfactory evidence of their repentance, or, at any rate, of not refusing them the consolations of religion in their last hour. The sterner party advocated excision.

The mind of the Church, after oscillating between these two courses, very decidedly inclined toward the compassionate one. The inclusive view triumphed over the exclusive, and those who were believed to be the truly penitent among the lapsed were taken back into the fellowship of the faithful.

But in two memorable instances—one after the Decian, the other after the Diocletian persecution—the Puritan party, those who were in favor of utterly refusing reconciliation, made a secession from the Church. They protested that it was an intolerable scandal to be compelled to eat with traitors. They would not live in fellowship with men who were willing to allow the Body of the Lord to be thus shamefully defiled. So they departed. They organized their separate communities, and having chosen their own bishops (for in those days even Puritans were Episcopal), declared themselves "the Holy."

And what was the result? The result was, in each instance, continued existence for two or three generations, ending in gradual dissolution and decay. In truth, these separatist bodies carried the seed of their destruction in their own bosoms. The exclusive principle that had moved them to rend themselves away from the fellowship of the Church, moved them, as fresh occasions of dispute arose, to rend themselves from one another, and so the rending process went on and on until, at last, there was nothing left to rend. Thus it must ever be with the working of the separatist principle in the Church. That principle tends inevitably to disintegration. One sect begets another, until gradually the original idea of a company of believers knit together in one organic body dies away, and nothing is left but the barren individualism, whose motto is "Every man for himself."

In Great Britain alone, the development of the separatist principle has engendered, it is said, no less than ninety different sects, and this enumeration leaves out of the account infidel organizations originally of Christian parentage, as well as the many of all sorts that must have worked themselves out, and died of exhaustion in times past.

Mystical interpreters of Holy Scripture have sometimes found in the seamless robe of Christ a symbol of his Church. The soldiers who crucified Him scrupled, it is said, to rend it. But we Christians, whom faith and love ought to have taught better, have done what they, with neither faith nor love, but only out of worldly prudence, refused to do. We have rent into a thousand shreds, to every soldier in the wicked conflict a part, that visible garment of light and beauty by which it was Christ's purpose that his spiritual presence in the world should be made real to men. It is hard to see how any single-hearted, humble-minded follower of the Lord Jesus can look with satisfaction on the spectacle.

"There can be no doubt that the presence of the Puritan spirit *in* the Church is healthful and desirable. There is need of a perpetual voice of warning against the temptation to obliterate the line between the Church and the world. The strictness of the Puritan is an admirable balance to the charity of the Catholic. It is when the Puritan passes from undervaluing unity into breaking unity that the harm is done. He goes out and establishes his rival altar. He makes, as he imagines, a new and cleaner church. And what follows? So long as the traditions of the quarrel can be kept alive, and the zeal of the fathers runs in the blood of the children, the sect preserves integrity; but by and by the original ground of the separation is forgotten, and the movement either changes its direction or runs out into nothingness like a river in the sand.

We have been considering the shortcomings of Puritanism as a polity. A parallel line of thought would show how the separatist principle also impoverishes doctrine. It stands to reason that the theology of a party—and every sect is by its very nature a party—must be one-sided. The founder of a "denomination" is generally a man who has a singularly clear and strong perception of some one truth of religion. This, the planetary center around which all his own thoughts revolve, becomes, as a matter of course, the pivot of the system he imposes on his followers. This cardinal truth may be the Fatherhood of God or it may be the Second Coming of our Lord, or it may be the importance of administering baptism in some particular way: whatever it is, the sectarian mind dwells on it to the exclusion of all else, so that gradually articles of the faith which, at the start, no one would have thought of disavowing, fall into the background and are lost.

Count the steeples in an American town. It is all very well to say that they are so many fingerposts pointing heavenwards. In reality, each is the representative of a certain portion of truth, torn out of its place in the perfect circle of Catholic doctrine, and mangled in the process. The Puritan theory, undervaluing, as it does, the importance of Church-life, forms a theology wholly subjective; and this, becoming gradually more and more attenuated, at last provokes men to exclaim with a sharp satirist, "Enough of this invisible Christianity!"

No one can ever know how large a proportion of our current infidelity is traceable to the disgust engendered in educated minds by sectarian narrowness. The thoughtful boy, coming suddenly to the knowledge that the ocean of God's truth is broader and deeper than the village millpond by which he was brought up, is often hasty to resolve that he will start upon the open sea in his own skiff, unpiloted, and with no compass but the stars.

The individual mind, however marvelously fashioned and endowed, is never competent to gather up into itself the full wealth of the Christian revelation; and a sect that does no more than reflect the thoughts of some spiritual giant of the past, is forever liable to overthrow at the hands of some spiritual giant of the present, possibly a child of its own begetting. Happy those souls that are content to rest in a truth larger than they can grasp, willing to "know in part," but not willing to call a part the whole.

V. Liberalism:
The Idea Distorted

SOME horticulturists are fond of forcing vegetable growth into gigantic forms. Others have the Japanese taste for cultivating dwarf varieties. With still others it is a passion to twist Nature into curious and grotesque shapes, compelling her, as it were, to caricature herself. In a word, the target of perfection may be missed in any one of three ways. A shot may fly beyond the range, or it may fall short, or again it may be, as we say, "beside the mark." In Nature's archery one of these errors gives us exaggeration, another diminution, and the third distortion.

But plants and trees and animals are not the only things that grow. An idea, a creative germ of thought, also possesses this strange power of taking increase. Not only so, an idea, equally with a plant, is susceptible in its growth to disturbing influences from without, and may be forced into departure from its normal type either in the way of exaggeration, diminution, or distortion.

Granting, then, that there existed in the mind of Christ a distinct conception of the nature of the new society He founded, it is evident that the idea might have been expected to undergo at men's hands these three forms of variation. In point of actual fact this is just what has occurred. In Romanism we have the Church-Idea exaggerated; in Puritanism it is belittled; in Liberalism it is caricatured.

Two of these misapprehensions of the full Gospel of the Kingdom have been already studied. There remains the third—Liberalism.

What is Liberalism? One might well wish to be excused from answering the question on the score of its difficulty. It is not a question that can be answered in a breath; and yet it must be answered, and that satisfactorily, before we can go on. The reason why it is hard to define Liberalism is because of the uncertain and indefinite nature of the thing itself. In dealing with Romanism and Puritanism, we had something tangible to handle, for Romanism and Puritanism are systems. But Liberalism is not a system. Its very characteristic is its want of system. Liberalism is a spirit, a tendency, a movement, a slippery something in striving to grasp which we seem to clutch the air. And yet, in spite of the subtle character that attaches to the word, every educated mind associates a meaning with it, and is sure that it stands for something that does actually exist.

Perhaps it will help us to ascertain just what Liberalism is, if we determine in advance what it is not.

First of all, then, let it be carefully noted that Liberalism is *not* the same thing as liberality. The two words furnish an instance of a curious law of language, according to which substantives of widely different character may be formed from one and the same adjective. Thus from "scrupulous" we make both "scrupulousness" and "scrupulosity"—the one a strong, the other a weak trait. "Prudent" gives us "prudence" and "prudery"—the first a quality we value, the second a quality we dislike. And so also the word "liberal" develops, on the one hand, into "liberality," a thing everyone admires, and, on the other, into "liberalism," a thing many persons distrust. Indeed, there exists between "liberality" and "liberalism" much the same kind of distinction that we observe between "liberty" and "license." Liberty is freedom subject to the control of righteous law. License is freedom declaring itself independent of all law. An advocate for liberty asks only to be free to do what is right. An advocate for license asks to be free to do what he pleases.

We are now ready for a definition, and can make it the more intelligently for having taken these preliminary steps. Let the definition be this: *Liberalism in religion is the spirit that is impatient of anything like authority, whether in the line of doctrine or discipline.*

Liberalism passes in society under various names, some of them very high-sounding ones. Thus we have "free-thought," the equivalent of the old-fashioned free-thinking; we have "advanced thought," we have "free religion," we have "the modern spirit," and the like. All of them are phrases dazzling and fascinating to a certain class of minds, but underneath them all there lies the disposition to rebel against authority because it is authority, and an eagerness to sacrifice upon the altar of spiritual freedom all that makes it worth our while to be spiritually free.

The battle cry of Liberalism is, "Religion without dogma, and a Church without a pale!" It is a popular shout. Dogma is one of the best-hated words in the language. Any man may cast a stone at it, not only with impunity, but with applause. Harmless enough in itself, the word has somehow come to have a very spectral and uncanny look in the eyes of the public.

And yet, when we sit down calmly and think about it, how can there well be any such thing as religion without dogma? A dogma is simply an article of faith received and held as certain. Now since a religion must, for its very life's sake, claim to be true, and since any undemonstrable truth, when once put into the form of statement, be it a statement of only three words, becomes dogma, it is difficult to see how a perfectly undogmatic religion is to be attained. It can only come to pass in one way, and that is by persuading men to preface every article of faith with a "Perhaps." If the world can be taught to throw all its religious thinking into the form of hypothesis, and to begin its creed with "I conjecture," instead of "I believe," the victory of Liberalism over dogma will be complete. No less a task than this, the advanced thought of our day proposes to itself.

Christianity, as a religion, rests upon certain alleged supernatural facts. Take one of the simplest and least technical statements of these facts we have. Let it be that short compend of first principles known as "the Apostles' Creed." From its opening sentence, where we confess our faith in an Almighty Father, Maker of Heaven and Earth, to those solemn closing words that tell of our belief in an everlasting life to come, there is not a single affirmation which Liberalism, in some one or other of its forms, has not made bold to doubt. Indeed, Liberalism desires to treat all these points as open questions to be discussed, like the unsettled problems of science and philosophy, without the slightest semblance of restraint.

But the Church takes, and always has taken, a very different view of this whole matter. The Church accounts herself to be a custodian or trustee of what was at the beginning committed to her to keep. The very existence of the Church rests upon the revealed truths she holds like family jewels in her charge. Take away the facts in which Christians say that they believe, and the fabric we name the Church becomes at once no better than a tottering shell, unfit to stand against a breath of wind.

This constancy of the Church to her belief is a perpetual irritation to Liberalism. "What is this Church of Christ," it asks, "that she should presume to put a check or barrier to the absolute freedom of man's thought? Whence comes the authority that meets us with a 'Thus saith the Lord,' and bids us listen and

obey? Away with her! Away with her! She is an enemy
to liberty!" But when Liberalism thus cries out against
the Church, and demands the leveling of her walls
upon the plea of larger liberty, Christians have a right
to raise the questions, What is liberty? and Where is
liberty to be sought? An Apostle has given an answer
that will suffice for those who are themselves believers. This is what he says about it: "Where the Spirit of
the Lord is, *there* is liberty."

If there is any promise in the New Testament that
is clear and definite, it is the promise that the Spirit
shall be given to the Church. Before He suffered, our
Lord, in the most solemn manner, gave to his Apostles,
the then representatives of his Church, the assurance
that the Holy Spirit should be their constant guide and
stay. It was in the strength of this assurance that those
Apostles made bold to speak of the Church as a body
in which, as in a temple, the Spirit of God dwells. If,
then, it be true, as one of them avers, that where the
Spirit of the Lord is, *there* is liberty, and if it be also true
that, wherever else the Spirit of the Lord dwells, his
presence is especially and particularly promised to the
Church, then how can we refuse this plainest of infer-
ences that in the Church, and in the fellowship of the
Church's Head, true liberty is to be sought?

But it may be said that this conclusion is reached
only by an adroit dovetailing of texts for which Liberalism has small respect. The argument has weight with
those who believe the Apostles to have been taught by
God, but not with those who look upon the Apostles

as ordinary men, endowed with "a genius for religion." Granted. But let us see whether the same conclusion may not be reached by quite a different path.

A man complains that it cramps his liberty to be obliged to accept as certain and indisputable those great doctrines of which the Church has been the witness and keeper from the beginning. He should feel freer if those points were to be thrown open to debate. But suppose he has his wish: what kind of a freedom would it be? Begin with any one of the primal teachings of Holy Scripture. Take, for example, that all-important dogma with which the Creed already quoted opens: "I believe in God the Father Almighty, Maker of Heaven and Earth." This brief declaration, simple as it seems to be, admits of at least three doubts.

First, there is the possible doubt as to whether there be any God at all. The Scriptures themselves assure us that such a doubt has been entertained. "The fool hath said in his heart, There is no God." Here, then, there is room for one controversy.

Secondly, there is the possible doubt whether this Almighty Being, supposing Him to exist, possesses the attributes of a Father. Perhaps there is a God, but is He indeed God the Father? There are many facts in life that seem to militate very strongly against such a belief. It certainly is most difficult to reconcile the mysterious allotments of sorrow, pain, and wretchedness we see around us with any simply human conception of fatherhood. Here, then, there is room for another controversy.

Thirdly, there is the possible doubt as to whether God can in any proper sense be called "the Maker of Heaven and Earth." There are not wanting those who tell us that to look for any God other than the indwelling mind in Nature, the life-principle of the Universe, the immanent Spirit, is to grope after a nonentity. God and Nature are declared to be conterminous and co-eternal; and, if this be true, it certainly is an abuse of language to speak of One who has no existence apart from the heavens and the earth as being the "Maker" of them both. Here, then, there is room for still another controversy; making the third that can be evolved out of one single article of the faith, and that the very one which is least often called in question.

Now the ground that the Christian Church occupies is perfectly intelligible and distinct. The Church says, "This is the first article of our belief. We regard it as settled and unchangeable. We are ready to defend it, with the weapons of argument, against attacks from without, but we cannot and will not allow it to be questioned from within; for such a permission would be nothing more nor less than a breach of trust. The faith has been given to us to keep, and we must keep it, or else turn traitors to the Head."

The position of Liberalism is also perfectly intelligible and distinct. Liberalism says, "No matter where you got this article of the faith, it must come into the arena of discussion along with everything else. This is the age of investigation, and no belief is too sacred for our analysis. To draw the line *anywhere*, and say, 'Here debate must cease,' is to fetter and enslave free thought."

These being the respective positions of the Church and Liberalism, to which are we to look for the truest and best kind of liberty? Or, to put the question in another form, Which is indeed the spiritually free man—he who believes with heart and mind and soul in God the Father Almighty, Maker of Heaven and Earth, and who in the strength of this belief lives out his life trustfully and hopefully, confident that nothing possibly can harm him so long as the Sheltering Wings and the Guiding Hand are near; or he who, resolutely bent on keeping clear of what he deems the shackles of a definite belief, dwells all his days in a cloudland of uncertainty, a companionless spirit to whom God is "a feeling," prayer an absurdity, futurity a blank? Which of these two is the really free man? And where lies true liberty—on the side of the boasted Time-Spirit, or on the side of that other and better spirit, the Spirit of the Lord?

The question all lies in a nutshell. Error is bondage. Truth is freedom. If God has revealed truth to men in Jesus Christ, which truth without such a revelation could not have been discovered, is it not as plain as it can be that those who refuse to receive this truth are the bondmen, and those who gladly receive it the free? "Then said Jesus to those Jews which believed on Him, If ye continue in my word, then are ye my disciples indeed; And ye shall know the truth, and the truth shall make you free."[1] St. Paul's saying about liberty is but the scholar's echo of these the Master's words.

We have been considering the attitude Liberalism holds towards Christian Theology, strictly so called. Its attitude towards Christian ethics might be made the subject of a parallel inquiry. Theology and morality are sisters. To sunder them is woe to both. The one is religion looking God-ward, the other is religion looking man-ward. The connection between the creed of a community and its usages and customs is much more close than it is now the fashion to admit. The poet shows the insight of the philosopher when he affirms that

"Manners are not idle,"

for manners are morals, and morals are the fruit of principles, false or true.

The influence of Liberalism upon this human side of religion has been significantly pointed out by a familiar writer upon the history of language. "Full of instruction and warning," he remarks, "is our present employment of the word 'libertine.' It signifies, according to its earliest use in French and English, a speculative free-thinker in matters of religion, and in the theory of morals, or, it might be, of government. But as, by a sure process, free-*thinking* does and will end in free-*acting*, as he who has cast off the one yoke will cast off the other, so a libertine came, in two or three generations, to signify a profligate."[2]

The statement is undoubtedly too strongly put. "He who has cast off the one yoke" does not, as a necessary consequence, "cast off the other." The champions of Liberalism have often been, as individuals, eminently irreproachable in their lives. But the substantial truth of the writer's argument is not affected by this fact. Principles which a philosopher can hold in his study with no damage to his personal purity may prove to be poisonous leaven for the daily bread of a community. The multitude have wit enough to see that the same logical hammer that has destroyed the first table of the Law can also shiver the second, if they only have the mind to strike; for if nothing be settled about our duty towards God, it is an easy inference that nothing is settled about our duty towards our neighbors.

Certain it is that Liberalism, under all its forms, betrays a strong reluctance to recognize the guilt of sin. Sin is an error, sin is imperfection, sin is partial knowledge, sin is spiritual ill-health, sin is a misdirection of the will, sin is—anything but guilt. The race needs refining, that is all; and man may pray, "Lord, teach!" but never "Lord, forgive!" We find this "liberal" view of human guilt penetrating every department of modern thought. Thus we have historical writers like the late Mr. Buckle, proposing to formulate the laws of crime and reduce them to a system; poets of the animal order teaching that instinct is the only gauge of duty; pantheistic essayists defining evil as "good in the making"; and authors of romance justifying the outrageous vagaries of their heroes on grounds of physiological necessity.

It is now evident for what reason Liberalism was called at the outset a distortion of the Divine idea. A Church fiercely intolerant of dogma, while mildly tolerant of sin, is assuredly but a caricature of that clear-walled city built upon a rock, whose name is Holy.

The Catholic Church of Liberalism ought rather to be likened to the restless, passionate, tumultuous sea. And so it has been likened by one[3] whom the writer would by no means charge with ultra-liberalism, in a word-picture of marvelous felicity.

"This great rolling ocean, which looks up to God, is ordered by God, and obeys God, though each wave crest offers its own homage, each tide-surge worships in its own way! 'How lawless!' mutters the scientific theologian standing on the beach. 'What rebels!' cries the petty prince from some sectarian Heptarchy, as the disobedient tide drives him from his throne upon the sand.[4] But the great God looks on, and sees that there is no rebellion, and that there is perfect law. This ocean never rests. It pants, it heaves, or it throws up its blue waves till they crest themselves with white and faint away; or they pour on incessant, one infinite procession, to fling themselves in order against the shore; or they drop into a sleep which is not death, but breathes steadily and regularly as a sleeping child, and so in their calm reflect the blue of heaven; or they fling themselves higher and higher toward the sky, dropping down exhausted only to start up again with one effort

more; or, lying still beneath his sunshine, they deliver
to his demand the unseen vapors, which He transfuses
into delicious showers with which to bless the thirsty
ground. And in this rest or in that convulsion, tide-
wave, wind-wave, white crest, spray-dust, or unseen
vapor-cloud, each in its own beautiful service, obeys
one law of attraction, fulfills the word of Him who sets
it in order. That is the image Christ chooses to
describe his Church."[5]

Nothing in the way of rhetorical effort could easily
surpass this; but most readers will be a little surprised
to learn that the saying of our Lord's from which this
analogy between Church and ocean was drawn,[6] is the
following:

"For as in the days that were before the flood they
were eating and drinking, marrying and giving in marriage, until the day that Noe entered into the ark, and
knew not until the flood came and took them all away;
so shall also the coming of the Son of man be."

Most interpreters of the words of Jesus, St. Peter[7]
among them, have thought, naturally enough, that it
was Noe's preservation from the violence of the sea,
rather than the whelming of the unrighteous world
beneath it, that gave point to the similitude. It is the
Ark which is the Church, not the wild waters on which
the Ark floats solitary but secure. And yet this writer
finds in the deluge "the image Christ chooses to
describe His Church." God forbid.

The Catholic Church of Liberalism can consistently acknowledge no limits narrower than those that

bound the human race itself. "It goes below any one specific form of religion, and seeks to find the common ground on which all religions, or more properly religion itself, rests, and plants itself there. It contemplates the ultimate union, not only of all sects in Christendom, but of all religions, Christian and non-Christian in one."[8] To draw a line anywhere, and say, "On this side is the Church, on that the world," would be a proceeding fatally inconsistent with the first principles of Liberalism. It would be setting up a barrier, and a barrier is of all things the one that Liberalism most abhors.

Liberalism would make of the Church a vast, worldwide debating club; a society of which every man should be, in virtue of his birth, it member, and in which all questions touching either the Creator or his creatures, the past, the present, or the future, might be endlessly discussed and never permanently settled.

Now there can be nothing to prevent men from taking this position if they choose. Indeed, it is the only position that a denier of revelation can consistently assume. But when it is attempted to make it out that such notions are reconcilable with Christianity, even with a Christianity that has been watered down to its very weakest dilution, then it is time for those who believe that the Gospel is something better than a guess, and the Church of Christ something more than a contrivance of man's brain, to speak out and say so plainly.

The Holy Catholic Church is not a voluntary religious association formed by men for the purpose of freely handling the problems of human destiny. It is a family, a brotherhood, a household, to whose guardian care the archives of the faith have been entrusted. The members of this family have no authority to tamper with, to change or modify the sacred deposit given into their care. God's oracles are a trust. The generations before us held it for our sake; we are to hold it for the generations yet to come. And let it be held liberally, that is to say, generously and charitably, for we cannot err upon the side of too much love for men; and it is well always to remember that even "Jews, Turks, Infidels, and Heretics," although not of God's household, the Church, are yet members of that scattered family for "which our Lord Jesus Christ was contented to be betrayed and to suffer death upon the cross."

There is a short sentence in one of the most beautiful of the parables which gathers up with marvelous comprehensiveness the essentials of Catholicity, while at the same time it may serve to warn us against those very three perversions to which, as has been shown, the Church-Idea is subject. A glance at it will answer the double purpose of a review and a comparison, and may not inappropriately close the present chapter.

Our Lord is speaking in his character of the Good Shepherd, and after telling of his great love towards the sheep already gathered, He thus proceeds:

"And other sheep I have, which are not of this fold; them also I must bring, and they shall hear My voice, and there shall be one fold and one Shepherd."[9]

Take this prophecy part by part, and notice how the words, intended to apply primarily to his Jewish hearers, have also a lesson for ourselves.

"Them also I must bring, and they shall hear My voice." This may be understood as Christ's gentle expostulation with the spirit of Romanism. Rome has indeed heard his voice, but she has heard and given heed to other voices than his, the voices of enchanters and enchantresses, that have led her away captive.

"One is your Master, even Christ," said Jesus to the Apostles, "and all ye are brethren." Had Rome cherished this word, the Papacy would not have been.

"I am the way, and the truth, and the life. No man cometh unto the Father but by Me." Had Rome cherished this word, saint-worship and Mariolatry would not have been.

"It is the Spirit that quickeneth, the flesh profiteth nothing." Had Rome cherished this word, transubstantiation would not have been.

"Drink ye all of this, for this is My blood of the New Testament." Had Rome cherished this word, the denial of the cup to the people would not have been.

Yes, it is because Rome has followed after other words than those of the Lord Jesus, that she has lost, or rather overlaid, the true idea of Catholicity.

Again listen to the Good Shepherd's voice: *"And there shall be one fold."*

This is his gentle expostulation with the spirit of, Puritanism. In his zeal for the well-being of God's heritage, the Puritan cannot bear to see the tares intermingled with the wheat. Whether the good grain suffers or not, these hurtful weeds must be plucked up, and that speedily. The one message to which his ears are always open is the command, "Come out, and be ye separate." As a necessary consequence, division and subdivision follow upon the application of this principle; the idea of the one fold is hopelessly lost; and presently, in the strife between a score of competing folds, it is no wonder that poor, simple souls find themselves bewildered and distraught. Not that Puritanism is wholly in the wrong; only as Romanism, in its zeal for the "one fold," forgets some things that the Good Shepherd says; so this system, which is practically the opposite of Romanism, in its zeal for *some* things the Good Shepherd says, forgets in its turn the value of the "one fold."

Listen yet once more: "*One Shepherd.*"

Here is the corrective to the error of the liberal extreme. The mistake of Liberalism lies precisely in this, that it is not contented with the "one Shepherd." It looks for, and it demands, other leaders than the Son of Mary. "The Christian Church," writes one who heartily believes what he says, "is not large enough for this independent, sturdy, vigorous America. A native religion, not fetched from beyond the seas, a religion universalized by the genius of American liberty, must yet supplant the narrow and cramping Christianity of the Churches." There spoke the true spirit of Liberalism. It is reconcilable with the idea of "One Fold," if we will only make the Fold as wide as the world, and give free play in it to all conceivable religions; but it is not reconcilable with the "one Shepherd," for to acknowledge unreserved fealty to Him is, in the eye of Liberalism, to put shackles upon the freedom of the soul.

True Catholicity holds all three of the requirements of the prophecy in faithful equipoise.

It listens to the Good Shepherd's voice. It is loyal to the idea of the "One Fold."[10]

It owns no other Master than the Christ Himself.

God in his mercy grant that no "native religion" ever supplant this one "fetched from beyond the seas."

VI. The American Problem

OUR public orators are continually reminding us that America is "the theatre of a grand experiment." When we modestly ask to be told what the experiment is, we have, to be sure, some difficulty in getting a plain and consistent answer. Some will have it that it is Republican Government which is on trial, others say the federal principle, others popular education, still others universal suffrage. But in truth the elder world is not wholly unfamiliar with these things. A Republic is no novelty in history, neither is a federation, nor yet public schools and ballot boxes.

The peculiarity of our situation really lies, not in the fact that we have unexpectedly come into possession of a new stock of ideas, but in this, that we are testing a novel combination of old ideas under circumstances peculiarly favorable to success.

Instead, then, of speaking of the American experiment, it might be wiser to say the American experiments. Indeed, there is nothing to which our country

may be better compared than a great working labora-
tory, where a host of students are busily engaged, each
on his own separate investigation. Crucibles of every
shape and size are on the fire, retorts are steaming,
solutions crystallizing, blow-pipes hissing in all directions. Who is to collate the notebooks of the various
analysts, and draw out in a finished form the results of
discovery, if any discovery there be, another age must
determine. At present all is activity and bustle. Each
experimentalist firmly believes himself to be upon the
scent of truth, and it is hard to persuade any one of
the number that possibly his neighbor's line of inquiry
may be as important as his own.

Under these circumstances the present writer may,
without apology, boldly claim that the experiment of
greatest moment now in progress here is not popular
government at all, but this, *The mutual independence of
Church and State.*

We have dissolved a partnership which for fifteen
hundred years the world held sacred. Never since the
short period between the Edict of Milan (A.D. 313)
and the Council of Nice (A.D. 325), has the religion
of the cross found itself in circumstances at all parallel to those that environ it here and now. How this
state of things has come about, a quick review of the
past will show.

During the first two centuries of her existence the
Church of Christ occupied the position of a despised
and persecuted sect. In the third century she was still
oppressed, but at the same time less despised than

feared. Early in the fourth century State persecution ceased, and that far more deadly enemy to the Church's health, State patronage, began. It was in the person of the Emperor Constantine that the idea of an alliance between Church and State was first embodied. Ever since his day that alliance has been under one form or another perpetuated throughout Christian Europe. Whether the grim saying of Hobbes that the Papacy is only "the ghost of the old Roman Empire sitting crowned upon the grave thereof" be true or not, it is worth remembering that at Rome was struck the treaty which through all these centuries has welded Church and State.

But the conviction of the necessity of such a compact, or at least of its great value, has by no means been confined to the Roman Catholic section of Christendom. At the time of the Reformation the countenance and aid of the State was sought with perhaps equal zeal by both parties. Neither side was quite ready to disclaim the assistance of the arm of flesh. Rome, since she left the Catacombs, had always leaned more or less heavily on that support, and the leaders of the reforming movement feared that without some such shelter the fruits of their victories would be insecure.

Accordingly, at that momentous epoch there sprang up all over Protestant Europe those forms of national religion known as "Establishments," and through them the various governments undertook to guarantee to their subjects the benefits and privileges of pure Christianity. The establishments took shape according to the temper and bias of their framers. In some of them the principle was accepted that the Church is a society subject to the State, and the creature of its laws. This view of the matter degrades the Christian ministry to the level of what has been satirically called "a moral police."

In our mother country, the better ground was taken that the Church is a society distinct from the State, capable of entering into partnership with it, but still retaining, even during the continuance of the compact, a separate identity.[1]

But ever since the day when these adjustments were first determined, the mind of Protestant Christendom has chafed and fretted under them. Spiritual men have felt the truth of our Lord's saying, "My Kingdom is not of this world,"[2] and have perceived the impolicy, as well as the difficulty of administering under the same forms and usages the things of Caesar and the things of God. An impulse in the same direction has come also from those who are hostile to the Christian faith, and who desire nothing so much as to see the last of the Church of Christ. They are willing enough to have her die an easy death. Perhaps they would rather prefer that her end should not be violent. But gently or roughly she must somehow be put out of the way, and the first step toward this end seems to them to be the withdrawal of Government support. In the event, it may be seen, that so far from being put out of the way, the Church, when rid of that entangling friendship of the world which is "enmity with God," is more *in* the way than ever.

To these opposite but conspiring causes it is due that there exists throughout Europe today a growing public sentiment in favor of the abolition of the union between Church and State. Among Roman Catholics, this sentiment takes the shape of opposition to the temporal power of the Pope. With Protestants, the cry is "Disestablishment." Substantially, it is one and the same thought that is seething in the minds of both communions.

But it is to be remembered that in our own country this public sentiment has been anticipated by about one hundred years. Here in America we have the accomplished fact before our eyes. One of the earliest fruits of the Revolution, and certainly one of its most noteworthy results, was the declaration contained in the first amendment to the Constitution of the United States:

"Congress shall make no law respecting an establishment of religion."

In this short sentence lies wrapped the secret of our national destiny, and on the wisdom or unwisdom of this decision of the fathers hinges the well-being of their children's children. This is a strong statement; some will be disposed to call it a wild one. The popular mind judges the comparative importance of issues by the noise that is made over them, and because less is said and written about our religious, than about our political future, it is very generally supposed that the former will take care of itself. But in reality, slow as men may be to admit it, the religious vastly overtops in dignity and in import the secular question. History, like nature, works some of its grandest processes in silence; and even if no single word of prophecy were lifted, it would still be true that our destiny as a people is to be mainly determined by the mould into which our Christianity shall be cast.

Let us not shrink, then, from facing one of the first conditions of the American problem, which is this, that our Government rests in theory, and must eventually rest in practice, upon a purely secular basis.

We are as yet a Christian people, and we have a right to say that we live in a Christian land, simply because the majority of the population are nominally of the Christian faith. But we have no right to say that we live under a Christian government, for Christ and his religion are alike unknown to that instrument which alone gives the government its authority—the Constitution of the United States.

To be sure, there never has been any civil government in the world that has fully deserved the epithet "Christian," for the plain reason that there never has been a government willing to incorporate the golden rule into the law of nations. But then, a great many governments have been anxious to be considered Christian; they have professed allegiance to the Christian faith, and in a degree at least, have lent themselves to the support of Christian ideas. Our government does not even care to be reckoned Christian. It cannot be called an irreligious government, for it permits religions of whatever sort to go on their way unmolested, so that they refrain from molesting others. But a Christian government ours certainly is not, for there is nothing in its structure to prevent Infidels, Jews, or Mohammedans from administering it throughout.

There still linger among the usages of our governmental system some traces of the old concordat between Church and State. Houses of Congress, local legislatures, and courts of justice are opened with prayer. The Bible is more or less read in the public schools. Presidents and Governors issue annual Proclamations of Thanksgiving to Almighty God. Chaplains are appointed in the Army and Navy. On one of the less precious of our coins are stamped the words, "In God we trust."

Many persons take comfort from the thought that these things indicate a certain Christian complexion still clinging to the Government.

It is a feeble solace. These vestiges of Christianity, as we may call them, are printed on the sand. The tide has only to crawl up a few inches further to wash them clean away. There is nothing in the theory of the Republic that makes such usages an essential part of the national life. They rest for the most part upon the precarious tradition of colonial days; or if on statute law, what is statute law but the creature of temporary majorities? The moment popular opinion sets against them, all these relics of an established religion must go by the board. They are not the natural fruit of our system; they are but reminders of all old order of things that has passed away; fossils imbedded in the rock on which the existing structure stands. One by one they will probably be chipped out and set aside as curiosities.

If anyone doubts the soundness of this reasoning, nothing is easier than to put it to a crucial test. Suppose it should come to pass, through the silent working of commercial and industrial causes, that the majority of the population in some one of our States should be unexpectedly found to be non-Christian, and not only non-Christian, but strongly anti-Christian. Such a supposition is certainly in these days an admissible one. Now, would the Governor of such a State, being himself a Christian, have any right to issue a proclamation calling upon the people to assemble on a given day and render thanks to God "through Jesus Christ our Lord"? Or, to make the case still clearer, would he have the right to do this in the face of a protest signed by a majority of the voters of the commonwealth? No. The very first principles of our social system forbid it. The Christian minority would have to succumb in such a case without delay. We have no right to accept the law of majorities when it makes for us, and reject it when it makes against us. But it may be said that the magistrate, as a Christian, is bound to use his utmost efforts to bring the unbelieving community to a better mind. So he is bound, no doubt; but it is as a private Christian citizen, and not as a magistrate, he must do it. He cannot convert the population by proclamation. Nay, natural justice forbids that he should even try. Any other view of the case must of necessity land us in confusion.

Some years ago, certain very sanguine persons set on foot a movement which had for its object the incorporation into the national Constitution of an article recognizing the truth of Christianity. It is too late. The stars in their courses fight against so forlorn a hope.

The truth is, theories of government reduce themselves in the last analysis to two, the paternal and the utilitarian schemes.[3] Under the paternal system, a government is responsible for the well-being of the subject people in all respects, socially, educationally, religiously. The very name we give the theory tells the whole story. Government is the father of a family. The father knows the children's wants better than they know them themselves. He chooses for them their sports, their studies, their companions, their prayers. With such a theory of government as this an established religion is of course easily and naturally reconcilable.

But it is otherwise with the utilitarian scheme. That credits the people governed with more robustness, treats them as grown men, and leaves it to them to decide for themselves what they will choose and what they will refuse. A utilitarian government professes to provide for the temporal well-being of all the governed. It professes no more. It cannot undertake to guarantee spiritual blessings, because people differ so very widely as to what those blessings are, and how they are to be secured.

Now we in America have chosen the utilitarian scheme. We have done it deliberately and with our eyes open. Unless we are prepared to agitate for revolution, and to tear our social order up by the roots, we must continue in the path to which we have plainly committed ourselves.

Moreover, it is evident that the drift of the whole civilized world is in the same direction as our own. If we determine to attempt stemming the current, we must count upon opposing not merely a national tendency. but an ecumenical one. Let us think twice before we make up our minds that this is necessary.

It may be that, in thus spending our strength upon a despairful effort at opposition, we should really be found fighting against God. For ought we know, this worldwide movement may have caught its impulse from his hand, and may be working out his purposes. Why take it for granted in advance, that no good can possibly come out of a mighty change of which we do not see as yet even the beginning of the end? What if the foundations of the American social system were laid by men who, as it is sometimes boastfully, and sometimes tauntingly, and sometimes mournfully declared were no Christians? An old restorer of temple ruins has reminded us that it is possible for our God to turn a "curse into a blessing."[4] The gifts of unbelieving minds were well employed, if they aided, albeit unwittingly, to clear the ground for the better upbuilding of Christ's Church.

And here lies just the point which the writer is aiming to bring out into distinctness. *The ground is cleared*—cleared as it never has been before. The Church has, at last, full freedom to do her best. Some may think that it is with a great sum she has obtained this freedom. Be it so, the freedom has hers, and for it she has to thank those who in the interest of secular government cut the knot of Church and State. Why, then, should we not as Christians frankly accept the fact that human government is everywhere renouncing its diviner functions, and see whether in this very abdication there be not a blessing hid? We ought to have faith enough in our holy religion honestly to believe, and boldly to say, that all it need ask is "a fair field and no favor." This amount of concession, if justice can ever be called concession, a utilitarian government cannot well refuse, and more than this we should be foolish to expect.

Now let us not fear to face the very sternest conclusions that can be fairly wrung out of our premises. It is true that no social theory is ever carried out in real life with rigorous logical consistency. But suppose this American theory should be so carried out to its utmost possible limit, what then? Government would become, in such an event, simply a machine.

The functions of this machine would be the preservation of social order, the protection of life and property, the settlement of disputes, the punishment of crime, together with such matters as the coinage of money, the collection of taxes and imposts, the granting of patent rights, and the transportation of the mails. But the more perfect you make this administrative mechanism, the wider does the gap become between Church and State. And it is well that it should be so. Mere living by clockwork cannot satisfy the aspirations of society, and therefore when men find that civil government has been reduced to clockwork and nothing else, they will look about them to see whether there be not some social organism capable of supplementing the deficiencies of the secular machine. This sense of want, this reaching after something better, it is the high and sacred duty of the Christian Church to meet. The food and drink that are withheld at the Capitol must be sought for in the Temple. The more thoroughly the State secularizes human life, the more earnestly ought the Church to labor to spiritualize and ennoble it.

Nor need there necessarily be the slightest conflict in this partitioning of functions. It may seem a terrible thing to degrade civil government to the level of a dead machine, but perhaps, when we have become accustomed to so regarding it, we shall cease to be shocked, for we shall then expect of government no more than we expect of a machine. Let it be understood that what the State leaves undone, it is the Church's recognized privilege to do. Under such circumstances we need not feel obliged to call the State

atheistic any more than we call a Jacquard loom atheistic. The State is simply non-theistic—that is all.

But it may be said that civil government can never
wholly free itself from a connection with moral and
even religious questions, and that in this fact lies a
fatal objection to the view here advanced. The adjust-
ment of controversies between man and man, and the
custody of the marriage relation, for example, must
always, in the last resort, be left to the State. With limitations, this is true but it is hard to see how the truth
of it at all damages the writer's argument. The State
exercised high moral functions in the days of Pagan
Rome,[5] and can exercise them again without assistance from the Church. There is an important distinction, often overlooked, between morality and
holiness, between crime and sin. With morality and
crime a non-Christian government is perfectly competent to deal. Of sin and holiness such a government
knows, and cares to know, nothing at all. It is the duty
of the Church to furnish the State with a high and
pure standard of morality, and then to leave with the
State the responsibility of conforming its action more
or less closely to this standard. If the Church has a
Christianizing influence on individual legislators and
judges, the results will of course appear in Christian
legislation and Christian judicature. But even supposing, what is most unlikely, that the whole machinery
of government were to fall into the hands of infidels,
the administration of justice and the enforcement of
the laws need not necessarily cease. There would still

be a social order, there would still be some enforced standard, however meager, of purity of life.

But is the Christian religion, as we see it in America today, prepared to take up, or able to carry the heavy weight of responsibility our national theory of civil government throws down at its feet? Is the Church of Christ so organized in this land as to be equal to the tremendous demand thus made upon her energies? We want a large-roofed, firmly founded spiritual dwelling place—a Home of God, a shelter for a mighty people. Can we have it? Does such a fabric anywhere stand ready? If it does, where is it? If it does not, is there any hope? These are questions which a believer in "invisible Christianity" will set aside at once as superfluous. "We have the desired structure already," he will say, "in the united hearts of all true Christian people, of whatever name or sect." But those who hold to the need of the "one Body" as well as the power of the "one Spirit" will take another view of the matter. To them it will seem that Christianity must be something more than a ghostly presence in the land, if it is to do the work mapped out for it. It must have hands and arms and feet. Between these members there must be harmony of movement, and over them unity of control.

We are thus brought face to face with the American Problem, which is this: Given a country constituted like ours, how is the Church of Christ therein planted to achieve and to maintain her proper unity?

If we would handle the problem successfully, we must first of all ascertain what are the exact conditions of it. That is to say, we must have a clear understanding both of the difficulties we may expect to encounter and of the helps upon which we have a right to count in our progress towards a solution.

As to the difficulties, they are manifest enough, and numerous enough; and if we thought we were working out the problem unaided, we might well be excused for calling them insuperable.

In the first place, we have a population more strangely assorted than any other at present comprised within the limits of a single nationality.[6]

Representatives of almost all the peoples and the faiths of Europe are on the ground in force. "Parthians, and Medes, and Elamites, and the dwellers in Mesopotamia" can scarcely have been more unlike each other in most respects than are the English, Irish, German, Italian, African, Chinese, and Indian elements of our motley census.

Then, too, it must be remembered that the three tendencies of religious thought which have been already reviewed under the names of Romanism, Puritanism, and Liberalism, exist here not merely as tendencies, but as organized powers, each zealously devoted to the work of pushing its own interests. Hence, it happens that every effort after a genuine catholicity is almost sure to fall under the suspicion of being a covert attempt at denominational aggrandizement.

But the conditions of the problem are not all of them discouraging. The believers in American Catholicity have food for hope. In weighing the significance of any given feature of national life, it is well to notice the counterpoise. That a marvelous diversity of origin distinguishes our population cannot be denied, but there is a fact of equal significance to be set over against it. Notwithstanding our strange mingling of bloods, there is one race that contrives to keep, and for obvious reasons always will keep the ascendancy—the Anglo-Saxon. Doubtless, the Anglo-Saxon mind has undergone, and in the future is destined still further to undergo, important changes here in America. But these changes have not been and will not be of such a kind as to alter the foundations of our national character. In our favorite virtues and our favorite vices, in our judgments and our tastes, we shall bear the impress of the Anglo-Saxon mint forever. The wars of the last century settled the question of ascendancy in America; and the failure of Napoleon III's attempt to gain for the Latin races a fresh foothold on our soil only put the seal to that settlement.

Our very language bears a constant witness to this great fact of history. Were we really as a people the conglomerate race we are sometimes supposed to be, we should at this moment bespeaking a miserable *patois* of English, Spanish, and Dutch. As it is, English is spoken in this country by all classes of society with a far greater degree of uniformity, and with fewer provincialisms, than in Great Britain itself. It is not easy to overstate the importance of this fact that we are an English-speaking people. By this weapon of language alone Anglo-Saxon ideas will be able to hold America against all comers. Nor is it difficult to see the bearing which this dominancy of race has upon our problem. The more thoroughly educated our people become, the more will they feel, through the medium of literature, the influence of those great minds that held England to her moorings in the day of the disruption of Western Christendom. This is not saying that Americans are destined eventually to conform to the present Anglican Church-system in its minutest details. That the writer entertains no such foolish expectation will, it is hoped, appear in due time. But what is seriously claimed is this: that certain leading ideas which in time past guided the men of Anglo-Saxon stock in the great controversy with Rome, will in time future guide the men in whose veins the same blood still runs. The Catholic Church of America will doubtless have something peculiarly American about its build; but at the same time it will assuredly bear a closer resemblance to an English home than to either an Italian *palazzo* or a French chateau.

There is another consideration, quite apart from this question of race, which must also be set down on the hopeful side in the discussion of our problem. Americans are an intensely practical people. Endowed with a large allowance of common sense, fertile in expedients, and prompt in action, they are not apt to be long tolerant of a proved absurdity. Only let the religious portion of our community become once persuaded that it is a palpable absurdity to call the existing jumble of denominations, followings, and sects Christian unity, and they will work night and day, and pray day and night, until something better is brought to pass. It so happens that there has been a great deal in the experience of our national life to make transparent the folly of calling disunion union, and disorder order. We have learned that for all practical purposes the unity of a people is dependent on the visible unity of its government. We have learned that the efficiency of an army is dependent on the thoroughness of its organization and the harmonious working of its parts. Now the Church is the People of God and the Army of Christ. It seems scarcely necessary to say more—the illustration enforces itself.

Thus much for the statement of the problem and its conditions. It remains to discuss the ways and means to a solution. This must be reserved for another paper. Meanwhile, one word of encouragement to those timid souls who can see nothing in the present state of things but chaos, and nothing in the future but despair.

It is written in a certain place that once, when the earth was without form and void, and darkness was upon the face of the deep, the Spirit of God moved upon the face of the waters, and God said, "Let there be light." Can it be that the breath which could thus mould and shape a formless universe is unable to give unity and order to a great family of living souls? Can it be that He who has promised his Spirit to the Church, will not at the right moment speak the word and lighten our darkness as He lightened that? It is the especial work of the Holy Spirit to draw unity out of confusion. Babel was man's work, but Pentecost was God's. Is it asking too much of Him who has bidden us ask what we will, if we pray that when the Church is "minished and brought low," God will at last bestow on her his inestimable gift of peace?

VII. Reconciliation

WHEN an intelligent man not wholly forgetful of the past of Christendom, nor wholly blind to its present estate, stands up in his place and solemnly says, "I believe in the Holy Catholic Church," what does he mean?

Does he mean that in his judgment the particular household of faith to which he is attached is, in distinction from and to the exclusion of all other communions calling themselves Christian, the sole depository and trustee of the blessings promised in Holy Scripture to the Church? He may mean this, and we must not too hastily refuse him his epithet of "intelligent" if he does. Some of the most cultivated and devout minds of modern times have given in their adhesion to this view, and we certainly shall not win them to any other by suggesting that in doing so they took leave of their senses. But is this exclusive interpretation of the language of the Creed the only one consistent with honesty and right reason? Might not our intelligent worshipper say, and in nine cases out of ten would he not say, that his faith in the Holy Catholic Church was largely of the sort defined in the Epistle to the Hebrews as "the substance of things hoped for, the evidence of things not seen"? If, upon making this confession, he were to be charged with pure idealism, with being a member of the Church of the Future, a visionary, an ecclesiastical Quixote, he could answer, "Nay. I gladly admit that the Church has an historical past as well as a possible future. Other foundation can no man lay than that is laid. I would not build upon a cloud. Only I must refuse to call the fabric perfect, so long as I see the ground strewn with stones evidently cut for the wall and waiting to be lifted into place. In saying, then, that I believe in the Holy Catholic Church, I confess to faith in a partly realized and partly unrealized plan."[1]

Whether this position be tenable or not, a strong argument in its favor might be drawn from a recent chapter in our national history. When in the darkest days of the long struggle between North and South, a man said, "I believe in the Union, and am ready to die for it," was there anything necessarily contradictory or inherently absurd in his confession of faith? There certainly was a seeming contradiction and an apparent absurdity. Almost all the outward and tangible evidences of unity had gone to the winds. In not a single State south of a certain boundary line was the authority of the General Government acknowledged. Foreign critics looking on declared, almost with unanimity, that the Republic was at an end. An English scholar issued the first volume of a ponderous work on the "History of Federal Government from the Foundation of the Achean League to the Disruption of the United States." And yet, in the face of all this, hundreds of thousands were found saying, and saying honestly, "We believe in the Union." Were they mad? To some they might have seemed so. The Union in which they declared their faith was certainly, for the time, most seriously broken. And yet, after all, those men were something better than mere dreamers. They had a foundation for their confidence, and they knew it. All was not swept away. The ancient Constitution stood. The continuity of Republican Government survived. The capital, too, with all its outward and visible symbols of legitimacy—the national archives, the halls of legislation, the seats of executive and administrative power—this remained. In a word, there was a center, a definite and tangible center, around which to rally. And thus, at last, what had seemed to be a hoping against hope, grew into fruition, and faith was justified.

Is the cause of Church unity in this country any more desperate today than was the cause of civil unity seven years ago?

In the earlier chapters of this book the question of Catholicity was discussed in abstract terms. This was necessary as a preliminary step to any satisfactory handling of practical issues. But we have now come down from the region of pure ideas into the denser air of everyday experience. We find ourselves face to face with the problem of Catholicity as it presents itself in this new world we call America. Here, if anywhere on earth, a Church of the Reconciliation ought to be among the things possible. Nowhere else can the constructive effort be made with so fair a promise of success. Religion is here, as we have seen, unhampered by any perilous alliance with the civil power; the atoms of social life are in easy motion, ready to be crystallized into almost any conceivable form; and if Christian unity without coercion is anything better than an idle dream, there is nothing to forbid our bringing it, with God's help, to pass. While, therefore, we seem to be narrowing the broad question of Catholicity when we thus fence it within national limits and subject it to local conditions, we are in reality only putting to the test principles which have an interest and an application as wide as the Christian world.

First of all, then, who are to be recognized as forming what may be called the constituency of the Catholic Church of America? Dare we give a narrower definition than St. Paul? He said to his Galatian converts, "As many of you as have been baptized into Christ, have put on Christ." Baptism with water, administered "in the Name of the Father, and of the Son, and of the Holy Ghost," with the intention of engrafting the person baptized into the Christian Church, does in itself confer citizenship therein. So the King decreed: so has the Realm received. The theology of Rome itself, strictly as it guards the pale of the Church, does not deny this privilege of birthright to any of the baptized, even though they may have received it from what is judged an heretical source.[2]

It may be objected that such a loose canon as this would turn the Church of the Reconciliation into an indiscriminate rabble. Thousands and thousands who care not a straw for religion could easily prove the simple fact of baptism. But it must be observed that we have not yet come to the question of discipline. It is one thing to have a right of membership in the Church, and quite another to be in the enjoyment of the privileges of communion.[3] The point under discussion now is what constitutes citizenship, not what constitutes good citizenship. We are considering how from an abnormal, we are to get back into a normal state of things.

Let us recur to the analogy of the civil war. The theory held by the General Government, from first to last, was that the people of the South, notwithstanding all that had happened, continued to be citizens. They were alienated citizens, citizens out of their right relations with their fellows, but citizens none the less, and as such to be treated. This was very different from the position taken towards the so-called State Organizations which these same alienated citizens had made. The supposed States were not recognized at all, or only in so far as certain amenities of war required it. In other words, while the right to construct new governments was denied, the inherent right of citizenship conferred by birth on American soil or by naturalization under American laws was admitted. By a similar reasoning it is perfectly consistent to deny the possibility of there being ten or twenty churches within the limits of a single nationality, while at the same time we admit that every individual member of these numerous societies has, in virtue of his baptism, a right of citizenship in the One Church Catholic of Christ. If it be asked—Why then fret ourselves about Church unity, when all the baptized are already members of the One Body? the answer lies in another question equally to the point—Why did we fret ourselves about national unity, when all, both North and South, were confessedly citizens by birth?

Starting from the broad vantage ground thus given us by a generous definition of Church membership, we have next to seek some one, well understood, central position fitted to serve as a rallying point for the scattered army of the Cross. The necessity of some definite center of unity is demonstrable. The way to produce a beautiful effect in crystallization is to hang up by a thread a solid piece of stone or metal in the liquid that contains the future crystal in solution. The minute particles, as they pass out of the state of solution, attach themselves to the stone or metal, and the final result is a marvelously symmetrical whole, in which the planes and points and angles seem all to have been arranged according to a preconceived idea. Similarly, whenever any social organization has become dispersed, or thrown into solution, there is needed for its recollection a firm core or nucleus about which the returning parts may group themselves. To leave the chemical and to revert to the architectural figure, the first condition of the problem of American Catholicity is a definite foundation. Moreover, this foundation must have an historical character; its roots must be driven deep down into the farthest past; it cannot be the creature today. It would be simply absurd to call a general convention of the baptized, and vote the Church of the Reconciliation into being. Politic parties and benevolent societies and religious sects can be made in that way, but a great national Church never. Something stronger than an improvised platform of principles is needed to hold up the House of God. Her spires and turrets soar forever into the clear air of the Future. Her foundations are upon the holy hills. She is built into and upon the Past.

Two religious systems, and only two, offer to the Christian people of this country an historical basis of unity. These are respectively the Anglican and the Roman Churches. Both trace their lineage to Apostolic times. Both are especially solicitous to retain the grand old epithet of "Catholic." Not a few thoughtful people are of opinion that between these and a third power, namely, Religious Liberalism, the real battle of our future lies.

But in this discussion about foundations, Liberalism may be cast out of the account; for whatever else may be said in its behalf, nobody pretends that Liberalism has any historical basis of Church unity to propose.

Here then are two churches, one of Anglo-Saxon, the other of Italian stock, each maintaining, and each maintaining truly, that it can offer to the American people an historical basis of unity. It is by no means certain that the nation will choose either of the two; but it is not hazarding much to say that if there is ever to be such a thing as a United Church of America, it will rest either upon an Anglican or a Roman foundation. It would be difficult to exaggerate the importance of the choice. To be sure, nothing is more common than for half-informed people to combine with ill-intentioned people in representing that after all there is not much to choose between these two foundations. Very many worthy Christians regard Anglicanism as only a modified form of Romanism—a Romanism robbed perhaps of some of its tinsel and glitter, and in a measure purified, but in its inner nature and essence Romanism still. And so, also, nothing is more common than to hear the case put as if there were really only two instead of three alternatives between which to choose.

"Atheism or Ultramontanism," said Lamennais, and there are many who delight to echo the sentiment on this side of the Atlantic. But we are not Frenchmen; and so long as we keep our eyes open, we shall not be snared by "the falsehood of extremes." When it has been proved that the Papal Supremacy, the worship of the Blessed Virgin, the invocation of saints, transubstantiation, the denial of the cup to the laity, masses for the souls in purgatory, indulgences, and the enforced confessional are matters of no moment, then, but not till then, shall we know that between the Roman and the Anglican positions there is not much to choose.

The truth is, Anglicanism is the only form of Christianity of which Rome is seriously and thoroughly afraid. In the national Church of the Anglo-Saxon she sees a plant of hardy growth, and one which all her blasts do not suffice to wither.

"We gave the Protestant religion five centuries to run," once said an ardent Roman Catholic; "three of the five are over, and before the other two have passed, the whole thing will be reabsorbed." Yes; three centuries have gone, but the Anglican Communion has not gone, and will not go. It never was more vigorous in a spiritual sense than now. It stands, as Wellington's squares of infantry stood at Waterloo, firm, patient, dogged, if we must call it so but true—true as steel.

We have come to a turning point in the progress of our argument, to a question in which all the lines of thought upon which we have been moving meet. It is this: What are the essential, the absolutely essential features of the Anglican position? When it is proposed to make Anglicanism the basis of a Church of the Reconciliation, it is above all things necessary to determine what Anglicanism pure and simple is. The word brings up before the eyes of some a flutter of surplices, a vision of village spires and cathedral towers, a somewhat stiff and stately company of deans, prebendaries, and choristers, and that is about all. But we greatly mistake if we imagine that the Anglican principle has no substantial existence apart from these accessories. Indeed, it is only when we have stripped Anglicanism of the picturesque costume which English life has thrown around it, that we can fairly study its anatomy, or understand its possibilities of power and adaptation.

The Anglican *principle* and the Anglican *system* are two very different things. The writer does not favor attempting to foist the whole Anglican system upon America; while yet he believes that the Anglican principle is America's best hope.

At no time since the Reformation has the Church of England been in actual fact the spiritual home of the nation. A majority of the people of Great Britain are today without her pale. Could a system which has failed to secure comprehensiveness on its native soil hope for any larger measure of success in a strange land?

But what if it can be shown that the Anglican system has failed in just so far as it has been untrue to the Anglican principle? And what if it can be shown that here in America we have an opportunity to give that principle the only fair trial it has ever had?

The true Anglican position, like the City of God in the Apocalypse, may be said to lie foursquare. Honestly to accept that position is to accept:

1. The Holy Scriptures as the Word of God.
2. The Primitive Creeds as the Rule of Faith.
3. The two Sacraments ordained by Christ himself.
4. The Episcopate as the keystone of Governmental Unity.

These four points, like the four famous fortresses of Lombardy, make the Quadrilateral of pure Angli-

canism. Within them the Church of the Reconciliation
may stand secure. Because the English State-Church
has muffled these first principles in a cloud of non-
essentials, and has said to the people of the land,
"Take all this or nothing," she mourns today the loss
of half her children. Only by avoiding the like fatal
error can the American branch of the Anglican
Church hope to save herself from becoming in effect,
whatever she may be in name, a sect. Only by a wise
discrimination between what can and cannot be con-
ceded for the sake of unity, is unity attainable. We will
make, therefore, the tour of the Quadrilateral.

1. The Holy Scriptures as the Word of God

Anglicanism is happily pledged to no special philosophy of inspiration. "It seems pretty generally agreed
among thoughtful men at present," says Bishop
Harold Browne, "that definite theories of inspiration
are doubtful and dangerous."[4] A like wisdom framed
the sentence, already once quoted in these papers,
"Holy Scripture containeth all things necessary to
salvation: so that whatsoever is not read therein, nor
may be proved thereby, is not to be required of any
man that it should be believed as an article of the
Faith, or be thought requisite or necessary to salvation."[5] No doubt the Bishop and the Reformer had
very different polemical purposes in view when they
wrote, but their words are in admirable accord,
notwithstanding. Holy Scripture, according to the

Anglican view, is the treasure house of God's revealed truth. How far and in what precise manner the divine and the human elements coexist there, it is idle to surmise, because manifestly impossible to determine. It is enough to know that in a sense peculiar and unique, differencing it from all other books, the Bible is God's word or message to us. The embassage of the Son of God is evidently the subject of the Scriptures. When the fact of this embassage has been once acknowledged, all difficulties about inspiration fly to the winds. To the mind convinced that the "Word was made flesh," nothing seems more natural than that God should have provided and protected the memorial of so transcendent an event.

But the Church must have some guarantee from its members that the cardinal truths enshrined in Holy Scripture are indeed received. Hence the necessity of a creed. It is simply trifling with words to say that the Scriptures are in themselves an all-sufficient creed. They are too voluminous to be grasped entire by any single mind, and even if they could be so grasped, they would not be a creed, for a creed is a summary of truths thought to be essential, and it has never been held that a knowledge of every minutest detail of Scripture is essential to the well-being of the soul. Scripture, like Nature, is a vast field of research. The creed is gathered out of Scripture, just as physical and chemical "laws," so called, are gathered out of Nature, that is, by the process of induction or the careful comparison of part with part. A man of science might as

well say that Nature is his knowledge as a Christian
that Scripture is his creed. Scripture is, in its way, as
inexhaustible as Nature. No man knows, or can know
thoroughly, either the one or the other. Hence the
dependence of the Church on:

II. The Primitive Creeds as the Rule of Faith

The principle of dogma is the cornerstone not only
of Church life but of all social life whatever. Dogmas
are simply first principles, and without some agreement upon first principles the very beginnings of
society are impossible. Some years ago of a Sunday
morning, a North German fanatic fired a pistol shot
at the officiating clergyman in one of the principal
churches of Berlin. He wished to put an affront on
Christianity, and he selected a man against whom he
bore no personal grudge as the representative of the
hated system. When subsequently arraigned in court
to answer to the charge of intended murder, the
criminal pleaded Not Guilty, on the ground that the
human will is the slave of circumstances, and that he
had done only what necessity compelled. Had the
judge condescended to hold a metaphysical discussion with the accused, it is just possible that the latter might have got the best of the argument. He
certainly could have cited not a few eminent philosophical authorities on his side. But instead of opening a debate, the judge promptly acted upon the
dogma, generally though not universally received,

that killing, or attempting to kill, is punishable, and sentenced the poor man to a term of twelve years' imprisonment.

What the axioms of morality are to the civil society, the State, certain primary beliefs or dogmas are to the religious society, the Church. It were as reasonable to ask the Church to dispense with the one, as the State to dispense with the other. Christianity, as a religion, rests upon a basis of alleged fact. Discredit this foundation, destroy people's confidence in its strength, and the whole fabric will tumble to the ground in a hundredth part of the time it has taken to rear it. When the Church renounces the principle of dogma, she will simply be committing suicide.

But granting the necessity of a creed, what ought to be the characteristic features of it? Conspicuously these three: Brevity, Definiteness, and Antiquity.

The Creed of Christendom must be short. This is equally a necessity, although on different grounds, for the learned and the unlearned. The least educated require a brief confession of faith, because it is unreasonable to expect them to carry a long one in their minds. The most highly educated require the same, because it is only upon a few points that any large number of trained intellects can ever be brought to an agreement. The more the human mind is cultivated, so much the greater power does it acquire of drawing subtle distinctions and defining delicate shades of difference. A creed that enters into a great number of minute particulars is a creed that invites opposition and makes conflict inevitable.

The early Fathers and Doctors of the Christian Church seem to have been profoundly impressed with the soundness of this position. It was not for lack of ability to frame elaborate statements of theological truth that they refrained from doing so. Familiar as they were with the refinements of the Greek philosophy, they might easily have contrived an intricate and highly subtilized creed had they wished. But their wisdom forbade it. They would not turn the Church of the Reconciliation into a Church of the Alienation, and so they kept their creed simple and short.

But as the years went on the passion for accumulating dogma grew strong. New controversies provoked new definitions, and new definitions newer controversies. Finally, as the sun went down on the great battle of the Reformation, both the contending parties entrenched themselves in very extended doctrinal earth-works: the Roman Catholics in the Decrees of the Council of Trent, and the Creed of Pope Pius IV; the Protestants in such symbolic documents as the Augsburg Confession, the Heidelberg Confession, the Westminster Confession, and the XXXIX Articles of the Church of England. The time has come to exchange these long-drawn creeds for the briefer rule of faith that satisfied the early Church. The exigencies of the sixteenth century may have demanded complexity, but the exigencies of the nineteenth demand simplicity. The Church is in the heat of a tremendous conflict, and her great need is concentration of force. We may learn a lesson in this matter from the striking change that has, of late years, come over the methods of naval warfare. Contrast an old-fashioned line-of-battle ship, a three-decker carrying seventy-five or a hundred guns, such as you might see in a picture of La Rogue or Trafalgar, and one of our modern iron-clads, with its two or four or six ponderous pieces of ordnance. To a wholly inexperienced eye, looking at the two in open ocean, it would seem as if there could be no comparison in point of power. How can that low-lying, unpretentious, scantly-armed ship stand for a moment against the huge Queen of the Sea, with her overhanging walls of oak, her triple row of cannon, her eight hundred men? But power is with the few, in this case. One single shot from the less conspicuous but compacter ship, will, if well directed, do more execution than a whole broadside from its many-mouthed opponent. The moral of the fable is not far to seek. The great doctrinal need of our times may be compressed into a single maxim: *Heavy guns and few.*

But let both parts of the maxim be kept equally in mind. It is folly to diminish the number of the guns unless at the same time we increase the weight of the metal. Dogma, well defined, sharply cut dogma, is, as has been already said, essential to the very existence of the Church, and just in proportion to the fewness of the required articles of faith ought to be their distinctness. The great practitioners have been those who have cured diseases with few remedies, but they would not have been great practitioners had they used no remedies at all. Special sins are but the outcropping fruits of one all-pervasive sickness of the soul. We do not need as many medicines as there are sins to heal, but we do need such few remedies as have always proved themselves able to reach the underlying cause of the complaint.

Definiteness, then, is a second requisite of the universal creed, as indeed it may be called the first requisite in the religious thinking of our times. There is far too much haze, not to say fog, in the air for either comfort or health. Men crave certainty on some points, and they are not satisfied until they have it. And yet how much of the prevalent teaching leaves those who receive it shivering in the mists that cling about the mountain's sides, instead of leading them up into the sharp but clear air of the summit. The religious mind of today expects to be told, and is willing to be told, that there are few things it can know; but what saddens it and sickens it is to receive the message that there is nothing about God or heaven it can know for certain. By all means what we do hold, let us hold fast.

The only other needful characteristic of a universal Christian creed, besides brevity and precision, is the venerableness that comes with age. It is sometimes rashly said that reverence for authority is gradually dying out of the world altogether. Much that we see in contemporary life and manners would seem to give color to the gloomy complaint. But it cannot be.

Human nature puts on a variety of liveries in passing from one service to another, but itself it cannot change; and until human nature has undergone a radical revolution, making it other than it is, there need be no serious fear that the sense of reverence for what is venerable will ever wholly cease to show itself among men. The awe we feel in looking on an ancient building, the attachment we have for an old home, the peculiar value we set upon an early and tried friendship, these all bear witness to our instinctive preference for what seems to be lasting over what we know to be transient. In superficial matters we are fond of variety and newness, but in all that most deeply affects the real interests of life we value permanence, and whatever seems to prove or promise permanence. A creed that is to commend itself to the confidence, and not merely to the admiration of Christendom, must come backed by the authority of the ages. The wisest theologian alive cannot make such a creed to order. No assembly of divines, however august, can compile it today. It must be found, if found at all, among the inherited treasures of the Church of God.

Can it be found? Anglicanism says, Yes.

The "Primitive Creeds" are the two popularly called "the Apostles' Creed" and "the Nicene Creed." The Apostles' Creed is of unknown antiquity. It is one among various similar versions of "the form of sound words" which were in currency among the early Christians.

The Nicene Creed is that statement of received faith which was drawn up by the assembled Bishops

of the whole Church, as soon as the cessation of persecutions made it possible for them to come together
and bear witness to those things which had been
"most surely believed" from the beginning.[6]

These Bishops, it is to be observed, did not claim
the power of making dogma. They only set the seal of
their testimony on what they asserted to have been
always received in the Christian communities they severally represented.

In these Creeds, or rather in this Creed, for the
second is only a restatement of what is contained by
implication in the first, we find centred all three of the
attributes required—brevity, definiteness, and venerable authority. Both Creeds long antedate the rise of the
Papal power, and the origin of the superstitious beliefs
and usages against which the Reformation was a
protest. Hooker speaks of the first as "That brief confession of faith which hath been always a badge of the
Church, a mark whereby to discern Christian men
from infidels and Jews."[7]

Of the second it may be said that it differs from
the first chiefly in the more marked exactness of its
language with regard to the Sonship of our Lord Jesus
Christ. A truth which, to quote Hooker again, is "contained, but not opened in the former creed," is here
set forth in unmistakable terms. It would seem as if
the words "his only Son our Lord, Who was conceived
by the Holy Ghost," must be just as decisive of
Christ's true divinity as the words that follow, "Born
of the Virgin Mary…suffered, was crucified, dead and

buried," are decisive of His true humanity. But since there were some who doubted, the Nicene Fathers determined so to define the dogma of the Incarnation as to make it perfectly clear what they held to be the immemorial belief of the Church. Critics who stand, by their own confession, quite beyond the pale of Christianity have no difficulty in seeing that this dogma is really what distinguishes the Church from Judaism and Islam. Certainly we who stand within the pale ought to be thankful for a Creed which enunciates the central truth of our religion with a distinctness and emphasis that fifteen hundred years of controversy have not sufficed to blur. If to surrender the more technical language of Nicea is to acknowledge that the Apostles' Creed leaves the Divinity of our Lord an open question, then let us cling to the Nicene Creed while the world stands; for between Arianism and Humanitarianism there is no stopping-place, and between Humanitarianism and Christianity there can be no peace.

But some parts of the Nicene Creed are confessedly couched in language that is strictly theological, and by the unlearned is hard to be understood. Need a formal assent to these propositions be demanded of all Christian people indiscriminately as a condition of communion? Anglicanism says, and always has said, No. If there be any doubt in particular instances as to whether the Apostles' Creed is received in its true sense, then let inquiry be made and instruction given. But let not a humble-minded child of God be turned away from the Holy Table because the philosophical and theological bearings of the term "one substance" are not clearly understood.

In the Church of the Reconciliation no more ought to be demanded of the laity, on the score of theology, than an affirmative answer to the question, "Dost thou believe all the articles of the Christian Faith as contained in the Apostles' Creed?"[8] and no more ought to be demanded of the clergy than assent to the same articles of faith as they are more exactly stated and more fully expanded in the Nicene Creed.

It may be easily foreseen that this avowal will call forth two sorts of criticism, the one from those who think the concession too little, the other from those who think the latitude too great. "Why make any distinction between the faith of clergy and laity?" asks a friend on the left. "You do not seriously mean that you would relinquish the XXXIX Articles!" exclaims with undisguised horror another friend on the right. Let us deal with one critic at a time.

A distinction between the theological knowledge required of a clergyman and that required of a layman is reasonable, for the same reason that a physician is expected to have a more intimate familiarity with the laws of health than his patients have. There are very many interesting analogies between the two healing professions, and those charged with the cure (or care) of bodies have much in common with those charged with the cure of souls. But in no point is the resemblance more suggestive than where it touches this question of doctrinal knowledge. Everybody, educated or uneducated, is bound to have some acquaintance with what we may call practical physiology, the laws of temperance, sleep, and exercise. Without this knowledge he cannot live a healthy life. But a man expects of his physician something more than this. He does not demand that he shall be in general a healthier person than himself, but he does demand that he shall have a clearer insight into the causes of disease, and a greater familiarity with the treatment of it.

Probably the catholic creed of medicine, namely, such a statement of physiological principles as all well educated physicians, the world over, would be willing conjointly to subscribe, bears about the same proportion in point of length to the everyday creed by which men eat and drink and sleep, that the Nicene bears to the simpler Apostolic formulary. We cannot afford to dispense either with the science of the professional, or with the plain knowledge of the non-professional mind.

Turning now to the other critic, the writer would say in advance that he has personally no quarrel with the contents of the XXXIX Articles.

Anyone who believes the Scriptures to be the Word of God, and who accepts the Primitive Creeds and the Episcopate, must be indeed unreasonable, if with a choice between Bishops Burnet, Beveridge, Browne and Forbes as expounders,[9] he cannot assent to the Articles.

But the very fact that it has been found necessary under the Anglican System (notice the word is "system," not "principle") to allow the various standards of interpretation represented by the names just quoted, is in itself a strong argument against making acquiescence in so extended a confession of faith a prerequisite of ordination.

So long as men continue to use their minds upon the subject of religion, there will always be "systems of theology" and "bodies of divinity." The scientific mind is never contented till it has arranged and codified its knowledge. Were the XXXIX Articles to be obliterated tomorrow, men would still be classified as Calvinists, Semi-Calvinists, and Arminians, as Lutherans and Zuinglians, as Realists and Nominalists. Not until you have shut up such fountains as the "Summa Theologia" of Aquinas on the one hand, and the "Institutes" of Calvin on the other, can you expect the minds of men to run in wholly new channels of thought. But the question arises, What is the use of a formulary which appears upon its face to present one system of theology, but is practically made to cover three or four? Can we not do quite as well without it? Should we not be logically more consistent, and historically more Catholic, were we to return to the old standard of the Nicene Faith, and exact no more, no less, in the way of doctrinal assent from the clergy of the Church, than was exacted fifteen hundred years ago?

But it may be said that the Nicene Creed, if made the sole standard of orthodoxy, would be subject to an even greater latitude of interpretation than the Articles now are. This is unlikely, for the reason that the

Nicene Creed was not framed with a view to ambiguity. Doubtless there would be in a Church where only this Creed were required, very many schools of thought, more or less divergent; but certainly no one can pretend that the Nicene Creed leaves the doctrine of the Incarnation in the same plight that the Seventeenth Article leaves the doctrine of "Predestination and Election." Men may hold very irreconcilable views with regard to

"Fixed fate, free-will, foreknowledge absolute."

and yet subscribe the Article. They cannot hold seriously conflicting views with regard to the nature of our Lord Jesus Christ, and subscribe the Creed. Now the Incarnation is the fountain-head of Christian truth. If we believe that, we are certain to believe much more. A confession that "Jesus Christ is come in the flesh" enforces a recognition of the sad necessity that brought Him here. Faith in Him as our only Savior flows naturally out of our faith in Him as our God. While we are loyal to this dogma, there is no danger from the side of unbelief, nor so long as we are also loyal to Holy Scripture is there danger from the side of superstition.

But a positive advantage that would come from relegating the Articles to their proper place among other similar summaries of theological opinion is this: a serious stumbling-block would be taken out of the path of those who cannot approve in principle of so large a body of dogmatic statement. Why, for example, should a valuable man of great attainments in scholarship and piety be debarred the ministry of the Holy Catholic Church, because, while accepting *ex animo* the Nicene Creed, he happens to hold to a literal interpretation of our Lord's words, "Swear not at all," and cannot honestly assent to "Art. XXXIX. Of a Christian Man's Oath"?

Let the XXXIX Articles have all the respect that is due to the origin and history, and all the authority that attaches to similar symbolic documents of their era. Only let them not continue to be considered, what they have never been in reality, one of the essentials of the Anglican position.[10]

III. The Two Sacraments

A marked peculiarity of the Christian religion is the fact that while intensely spiritual in its motives and aims, it does not loose itself wholly from the material world. Socrates bequeathed to his disciples a doctrine, and nothing more. Christ gave his people a doctrine clothed. He linked the inner to the outer world, and asserted his kingship over both. The pendulum of philosophy swings ceaselessly between the extreme of spiritualism and the extreme of materialism. A greater than the philosophers brought into the world a religion which is neither a ghost nor a corpse, but a living body dwelt in by a living soul.

The Two Sacraments of Christ's appointment image forth to the eye his two all-comprehensive sayings, "Come unto Me," "Abide in Me." The one is the

Sacrament of Approach, the other the Sacrament of Continuance. Baptism answers to the grafting of the branch; Holy Communion to the influx of the nourishing juices that keep the graft alive.

Thus the sacraments are a constant safeguard against the danger of theologizing in entire forgetfulness that we are in the body and on the earth, a danger which would seem in advance improbable enough, but which history teaches to be real. And conversely it is true that when men have made up their minds that Christianity is only one mode of speculative thought, a philosophy in disguise, their very first step is to disown the sacraments.

But the peculiar claim of the sacraments to rank as pledges of unity is this, that they are among the few undisputed legacies of the Apostolical age. Upon whatever other points Christians may differ, they are agreed that these two simple rites, Baptism and the Supper of our Lord, have been in use in the Church since the beginning. Even those who, like the members of the Society of Friends, reject the sacraments altogether, do so upon the ground that Christians have no longer need of such external helps, not upon the ground that the rites themselves are of post-apostolic origin. But without the sacraments the Church becomes a phantasm, and it is impossible to frame any scheme of reconciliation that shall dispense with these institutes of Christ's appointment, or leave the use of them optional with individual believers. The sacramental element is an integral portion of the Church-

Idea, and cannot be cut away with safety. But Anglicanism, while perfectly clear upon this point of the essential character of the sacraments, is not pledged to any particular theory of their operation. As in the matter of the inspiration of the Holy Scriptures, so here, it is the fact, and not the philosophy of the fact, that Anglicanism aims to grasp. Grant first that the sacraments are of perpetual and binding obligation, and secondly that they are channels of blessing to the Church, and the Anglican principle is satisfied. A transcendental theory about the way and means whereby the Spirit through Baptism brings us into God's Household, or through Holy Communion feeds us on the Body and Blood of Christ, is not required.

Hence it would seem to be a hardship for men to be driven into schism, or kept in schism, because their consciences are offended by certain phrases, other than the New Testament formula, employed in the administration of Baptism. Whatever may be our estimate of the importance of sacramental privileges, there can be no question that the validity of Baptism lodges in the act itself, not in the forms of words that may be employed before or after the act. The higher the view we take of the dignity of the sacrament, the clearer does this point become, so that, indeed, the unreasonableness of exacting conformity to one particular devotional formulary of Baptism, as a condition precedent of Church unity, may be said to be parallel to the unreasonableness of demanding that any one mode of administering the sacrament, such as immersion, aspersion, or affusion, shall be held valid, to the exclusion of all others.

But a far more serious difficulty than this besets the question of the relation of Baptism to Church Unity. It is a tenet of one of the largest and most influential of the Christian denomination of America that little children, unable to speak for themselves, cannot rightfully be made members of the Church in Holy Baptism, or treated during their early years as Christian children. Here is a point of difference which obviously does not admit of compromise. To blur over the issue is simply to cry peace where there is no such thing. The theory that the Church is a community which in great measure propagates itself by Christian marriage, and preserves itself by Christian nurture, cannot possibly be reconciled with the theory that the Church can grow only by adult conversions from an unbelieving world.[11]

It would be clearly unwise to open and discuss in this connection the whole baptismal controversy. Still, it cannot be amiss to call attention to certain misapprehensions sometimes entertained, the removal of which may make the way of reconciliation easier.

The Church in receiving little children to Holy Baptism, does not, as it is often supposed she does, guarantee to them *unconditionally* the heritages of eternal life. She simply receives them, as our Lord received them, with a blessing. She treats them as members of a pardoned family, pardoned for Christ's sake, and needing to be taught both the happiness and the responsibility of their high privilege. She says, It cannot be that the lambs alone, of all the Flock, are to be refused the shelter of the Fold. It cannot be that in the School of Christ grown people are the only learners. And so she welcomes the little ones, promises them all the help that love, and care, and tenderness, and holy discipline can give, and then expects them, when the right time comes, "with their own mouth and consent, openly before the Church" to ratify and confirm what was done for them at the start. In default of such a personal acknowledgment, the privileges of Baptism become practically forfeit and outlawed, for only those who with their own lips have confessed the faith are received to the privileges of communion.

When the first Napoleon wished to signify his hope and his ambition for his only child, he took him in his arms while yet an infant, and holding him up before the assembled legions of the Old Guard, caused him to be declared and made a member of that veteran corps. There was a profound meaning in the act. Thenceforth the destiny of the baby king was, humanly speaking, determined. He was to be a soldier, as his father had been before him, and from that moment the soldier life was to begin. Play, dress, studies, companionships, all were to be chosen with this definite future in view. True, the child appreciated nothing of the solemnity and import of the ceremony. His eyes and thoughts dwelt only on the burnished arms, the gaily colored trappings, the waving banners. Nevertheless, that was a moment of crisis for the little

King of Rome. In spite of his unconsciousness, a thing was done for him he never wholly could undo.

The Church, just now likened to a family and a school, has also its resemblance to an army. The leader is invisible, the weapons are not carnal, the campaign is against a spiritual enemy, and yet the sacramental host is no shadowy, unsubstantial thing, but real. To enroll children in this army is to undertake that from the beginning of their conscious life they shall be taught loyalty, and exercised in the use of arms. Unlike Napoleon's boy, the baptized child may claim the promise of God's blessing on his warfare to the end.

But the real ground of objection to the Church membership of little children is to be sought in that view of Christianity which has been already criticized under the name of Puritanism. The issue is between the inclusive and the exclusive theories of the nature of the Church. If, as the Puritan maintains, only a portion of the human race is salvable, and therefore only certain individual members of any given community are to be accounted subjects of Divine grace, then it is manifest impiety to assert indiscriminately of all infants brought to Baptism that they are therein made members of Christ, children of God, and inheritors of the Kingdom of Heaven. But the Church-Idea presupposes a whole world redeemed—not necessarily a whole world finally saved—rather a whole world put in the way of salvation. We may not presume to anticipate the awards of the Judge. We know not how many or how few are to inherit eternal life. Christ discouraged inquiries upon that head. But this we do know, that forgiveness may be had today by all who care to claim it. We come into the world the members of a guilty, but at the same time a pardoned race. To convince us of the guilt, to make us appreciate the pardon, this is the conjoint work of the Spirit and the Bride.

In a word, the Church treats redemption as a universal fact, and Baptism as a universal privilege. To bring little children to baptism is, in the Church's view, just as reasonable and natural a thing as for a man who has been in rebellion to claim for his family as well as for himself the benefits of a published amnesty.

When God made his covenant with Abraham, and founded the old Jewish Church, He gave an express command that the little children should be taken into it. Is it a fair inference from the silence of the New Testament that under the more generous vision of Christ's better covenant the little children are to be shut out? On the contrary, may we not argue that if the Christian Church had been meant to differ from the Jewish in so important a regard, we should have been told so and that therefore the absence of the prohibition amounts virtually to a positive command?

It is a curious circumstance that the opposition to infant Church membership comes from two sources as diverse and opposite as they well can be. On the one hand it is said, You must not bring up children as Christians, because you have no right to interfere with the spontaneous development of their religious natures. You must wait and let them decide for themselves, as if the question were opened for the first time whether they will choose the religion of the Bible or some other religion. On the other hand it is said, You must not bring up children as Christians because they cannot possibly be Christians until they have passed through such religious experiences as are only possible to persons of some maturity of character and knowledge of the world. They must sin consciously, repent consciously, and consciously be justified, before you have any right to call them Christians. But the objection, from whichever side it comes, is amply met by Scripture and by common sense; Scripture saying in a very positive way, "Train up a child in the way he should go, and when he is old he will not depart from it"; common sense assuring us that it is vain to say we will not educate our children religiously, since it is quite certain that if we do not educate them into Christianity, we educate them out of it. "Free Religion" can ask no better field for its maneuvers than an unbaptized community. At any rate, one thing is certain: the inclusive and the exclusive theories of Church life cannot both be true. They part company at this initial point of Baptism, but their divergence does not end here. If one is right, the other is Wrong. It is for this nation to choose between the two.

Turning now from the Sacrament of birth to the Sacrament of nourishment, we have to ask what place the Holy Communion ought to occupy in the Church of the Reconciliation. Certainly no subordinate rank can well be assigned to the only habitual observance our Lord by express command enjoined upon all the faithful. It is a wonderful thought that while empires have had time to be born and live and die, and whole civilizations have changed their face, this touching tradition has been kept, that on the night in which He was betrayed, "He took bread, and when He had given thanks, he brake it, and gave it to his disciples, saying, Take, eat, this is My body, which is given for you. Do this in remembrance of Me." And this in remembrance of Him have ten thousand times ten thousand and thousands of thousands done during the long tract of years across which we look backward to that night.

Weighing the fact apart from its religious associations and as a mere phenomenon of history, is it not perfectly marvelous that so slender a plant should have survived the storms and floods that have swept many another seemingly more stoutly rooted growth from off the earth? It cannot be a matter of surprise that Christians should love to regard an observance thus hallowed as being their supreme act of worship.

In defining the standard of fitness for the Holy Communion, the Anglican principle demands a close adherence to the language of Scripture, and a careful avoidance of the two extremes of harshness and laxity. It refuses to fence the Sacrament with the mechanical contrivance of the Confessional, a thing unknown to Apostolical times. On the other hand, it guards against degrading the sacred feast to the level of a mere sentimental observance, in which anyone who feels the momentary impulse may take part. "*But let a man examine himself, and so let him eat of that bread and drink of that cup.*" "*Draw near, ye who do truly and earnestly repent you of your sins, and are in love and charity with your neighbors, and intend to lead a new life, following the commandments of God, and walking from henceforth in his holy ways; draw near with faith, and take this holy Sacrament to your comfort.*" Such are the simple but searching tests of fitness by which the Anglican principle is willing to abide. They do not repel from the Lord's Table those whose very humility constitutes their best claim to a place there; nor yet do they make light of those important requisites—faith, penitence, and charity—without which no man may worthily partake.

The Holy Communion ought to be, more than it anywhere is at present, a guarantee of purity of character. The worst deficiency of American religion today is the want of a warmer interest in that old-fashioned occupation, holy living. There is scarcely a congregation in the land in which every one of the Ten Commandments is not literally broken. Give us back something of the "primitive discipline" of which the English Prayer book says that its restoration is "much to be wished," rather than allow the World utterly to swamp the Church. It were a fatal objection to the "inclusive theory" of the Kingdom, could it be proved to involve a universal tolerance of sin. While we guard against the narrowness of the Puritan, and refrain from bringing in our brother guilty in things indifferent, we have need to see to it that we maintain a high standard in things not indifferent, and keep God's pearls for others than the swine.

IV. The Episcopate as the Keystone of Governmental Unity

The Anglican principle insists upon governmental unity as an essential condition of oneness in the Church. Let us look at the reasons for this.

Headship is God's law. Double- and triple-headed creatures are monsters that exist only in fiction, or, if born, are only born to die. From its fountain in the bosom of the Holy Trinity, this principle of headship flows downward through all the ranges of created life. We find it in the constitution of the Family, recent social theories to the contrary notwithstanding. We find it in the constitution of the State, which, when it falls into anarchy (or headlessness) ceases to be. We find it in the constitution of the Church, of which God's only Son our Lord is Head.

But it is asserted that because Christ's Headship of the Church is invisible, therefore there can be no necessity for governmental unity within the Church itself. This is as much as to say that because the general-in-chief stands apart, withdrawn from the sight of his men, while the battle which he has planned and which he really directs is waging (like Moltke winning Sadowa at Berlin) therefore there need be in the ranks no subordination, no harmony of discipline, no one system of control. True, the Head of the Church is invisible, but the army of which He is the Head is not, and if ever any army needed unity, this one does. The enemy against whom we fight, divided upon almost every other point, is at one in hostility to Christ. Forces that can agree in nothing else, agree in hating the religion of the Cross; and whenever the cry goes up for an assault on that, they move in unison. We have need of the like wisdom in organizing for the defense.

The writer must be pardoned for recurring so often to this similitude of an army. He has done it for two reasons: first, because army life and its necessities have of late been brought so vividly before the eyes of the people that any illustration drawn from that quarter is sure to be appreciated; and secondly, because there is no argument from analogy that has been so lamentably perverted in the interests of sectarianism as this very one.

Just as an army, they tell us, is made up of companies, and regiments, and brigades, and divisions, and corps, and just as these bodies are of differing sizes and variously assorted as to their uniforms and weapons and modes of drill, so the visible Church of Christ on earth is composed of an indefinite number of sects or denominations, all engaged in the same warfare, but variously equipped, variously armed, and variously maneuvered. This is a fair statement of the sectarian argument, and as such is familiar to every reader.

But there is another way of putting the question, which is, to say the least, quite as strong. What army ever won a battle when every division and every regiment and every company carried on the fight each according to its own discretion?

The allied forces at Waterloo were composed of English, Dutch, Belgians, Brunswickers, and Hanoverians, not to mention Blucher and his Prussians. Supposing these various contingents, pleading ignorance of one another's language and habits, had undertaken to fight on independent principles, after the guerilla fashion—would the tide of battle have turned as it did? Moreover, the comparison of the various arms of the service, such as the infantry, the cavalry, and the artillery to sectarian divisions is specially defective, for the reason that notwithstanding the great "diversities of administration" and "diversities of operations" that characterize these several branches, one general scheme of polity covers them all; they are officered upon one and the same principle, and, when massed for any definite purpose, they yield obedience to the same superiors. Indeed, the only difference between an army and a mob lies here, that in the one there is discipline and subordination and concerted action, while in the other Heaven's first law is set at naught.

Advocates of the sectarian principle would do well to be shy of this army illustration. In their hands the recoil is far more destructive than the discharge. A much better way for them, if they would preserve consistency, is to abandon the idea of a visible church altogether, and take refuge in such consolations as individualism can afford.

The Church may safely admit an almost infinite variety of ways and methods; she can allow and must allow for differences of character and temperament and taste; but she insists that this freedom of play is beneficial only in so far as it consists with a recognition of authority and a faithful obedience to law.

Thus far the argument for governmental unity has been mainly one of analogy, an appeal to the mind's native sense of the fitness of things. But this is not the only reliance of the Anglican principle. History has a word to say.

There exists a form of Church polity which can be traced back, century after century, until we come to the very confines of the Apostolical age. A characteristic feature of this polity is headship. The name of it is the Episcopate. "After we have passed the difficulties of the first century," says Gibbon, "we find the Episcopal government universally established."[12] What "the difficulties of the first century" were, Gibbon fails to state, and whether he referred to difficulties in the Church or difficulties in his own mind does not appear. His testimony to the high antiquity of the Episcopate is chiefly valuable, because he cannot possibly be suspected of a bias in favor of the Church. But whatever Gibbon's "difficulties" may have been, neither he nor any other historian has ever proved that the polity which was *universal* in the year of grace 100 is another polity than that which was established on the day when Jesus, going up into a mountain, called unto Him whom He would, and "appointed twelve."

The Episcopate, therefore, has a strong historical presumption in its favor—a presumption which nine-tenths of contemporary Christendom respect, and which must be wholly overthrown before any other form of polity can put forward a reasonable claim to general acceptance. At any rate, it is by the Episopate, as one of its four cardinal points, that Anglicanism stands or falls.

The reluctance of the American mind to accept the Episcopate as a basis of reconciliation may be traced to two sources. In the first place, there is an undefined, but very real and very general dislike of the phrase "Apostolical Succession." For some reason or other, the words are associated in people's thoughts with narrowness and bigotry. They are supposed to be the cloak of some strange superstition, bred in the unwholesome air of the dark ages. Opponents of the doctrine represent the advocates of it as ascribing to a Bishop's touch a magical power akin to that which was once thought to reside in the hands of royalty. But the writer cannot help thinking that, after all, the prejudice is more against the phrase than against the thing for which the phrase stands. It is certainly possible for a man to be a staunch upholder of the doctrine of the Apostolical Succession, while at the same time he is without a tincture of superstition or intolerance.[13] Indeed, if there be no such thing as the Apostolical Succession, if the Episcopate have no more claim on our regard than any other form of ecclesiastical polity, then the sooner Anglicans in America shut their church doors and burn their prayer books, the better; for they are only adding, upon insufficient grounds, one more to the sectarian divisions under which the land groans. But if they have in the Episcopate that which links them by an actual historical connection to the Church of the primitive times, then they ought to thank God and take courage, and do all they can by the removal of misapprehensions and disabilities and needless partition walls of prejudice, to make their inheritance available for the enrichment of the whole scattered flock of Christ.

The other source of distrust in the Episcopate to which reference was made is this: There is a latent suspicion among Americans that this form of ecclesiastical polity is not in harmony with "the genius of republican institutions." That such a prejudice should exist is by no means surprising; indeed, the marvel is that under the circumstances the feeling is not stronger. Our grandfathers identified Episcopacy with the British monarchy, and for the most part were thoroughly persuaded that bishops and kings were in unholy alliance against human liberty. It takes a long time for feelings of this sort to die. They get into the blood and stay there. But as the people of the country become better educated, and learn to extend their view of the past beyond the few generations which local tradition covers, they will see that the Episcopate, so far from being pledged to alliance with any particular civil polity, possesses a wonderful power of adaptation to all forms of social organization. Certainly no historical scholar will venture to affirm that the Episcopate has ever, for any extended period, been the willing slave of either imperialism or monarchy.

It is generally agreed that in the first age of the Church, bishops were chosen by the suffrages of the faithful, and then consecrated to their office and given authority to execute duties by other bishops who had in times past been similarly empowered. It is thus that the American Episcopate is perpetuated today. Our bishops trace their *consecration* to the Anglican Church, and through the Anglican Church to the Church of the Apostolical age; but they owe their *election* to the free voice of the people of their respective flocks, and exercise their authority in as strict conformity to constitutional law as a president or a governor.

It is interesting to observe, as one of the healthy fruits of the republican movement in America, that the Church of England, in this crisis of her destiny, looks across the ocean for an instance of a return to primitive methods in the selection of men for the Episcopate.[14] There is, indeed, a difference of theory between the Republic and the Church with regard to the origin of authority, but it is not a difference that need provoke the slightest conflict. We must distinguish between authority and power. All Christian people agree that the Divine Will is the ultimate source of power. "There is no power but of God." Authority is delegated power. The difference between the Republican and the Church theories turns upon the manner of delegating the power. In the Republic, the authority is conferred by the direct act of the people. In the Church, the people designate the particular person with whom the authority is to be lodged, but the authority itself is conferred by those who in their turn received it by transmission from the past. Hence States may be forever springing into existence anew; but a "new Church" is an impossibility. Now it is evident that these two theories of authority cannot coexist either in the State alone, or in the Church alone. But when Church and State are separate, thoughtful friends of their country may think it not unbeneficial to the common weal to have the two theories work side by side, each in its own sphere. Perhaps, like centripetal and centrifugal forces, they may serve to keep our social system in true equipoise.

And now the argument in behalf of the four cardinal points of the Anglican position is closed. The appeal has been throughout rather to first principles than to historical details. If full information be desired upon such matters as the history of the Primitive Church, the Roman Catholic, Presbyterian, and Unitarian controversies, the validity of Anglican Orders, or the Constitution of the American Episcopate, there are books without number that contain it all. But there has seemed to be wanting to the literature of this subject a brief and simple exposition of what may be called the philosophy of Church unity, and more especially Church unity in America. This it has been the writer's aim to furnish.

It remains to touch upon a few points that have thus far passed unnoticed.

Some readers have perhaps been surprized at not finding uniformity in the mode of conducting divine service reckoned among the essentials of unity. The omission has not been due to any lack of appreciation of the value of a liturgy. As a Churchman, the writer need scarcely say that in his own judgment this method of divine service is the only one fitted to insure that combination of solemnity, heartiness, devotional richness, and doctrinal fidelity which all Christians will agree ought to characterize the public worship of Almighty God.

Certainly if the Bride of Christ can without vainglory boast of her adornments, she must be pardoned for taking an especial pride in that clothing of wrought gold with which the devotion of the centuries has robed her. The Anglican Church is so closely identified in history and in the popular mind with a particular liturgy that she has been not inaptly called "the Church of the Prayer-book."[15] Apart from the usual arguments in behalf of liturgical worship with which everyone is familiar—such as these: that it gives the people a more generous share of the service; that it insures great comprehensiveness of intercession, and a systematic reading of the Holy Scriptures; that it protects congregations against crudities of thought, mistakes of feeling, and infelicities of expression on the part of inexperienced or undevout men (arguments all of them which must be allowed some weight)—apart from these considerations, great significance attaches to the simple fact that this method of worship was in

universal use throughout the Christian world for at
least fourteen hundred years. Extemporaneous public
worship is a thing of yesterday as compared with these
venerable usages of divine service, which are our
inheritance from the early centuries.

And yet, strong as is the argument for liturgical
worship upon grounds of expediency and fitness, there
are good reasons for not reckoning a strict uniformity
in this regard among the first principles of Church
unity. It is true that liturgical worship was universal at
the earliest date in the history of the Christian Society
of which we have any authentic post-Scriptural record.
But it is equally true that the liturgies of that age
existed in wonderful variety. Upon this point all schol-
ars are agreed. Indeed, so numerous were the early
formularies of worship that they can be distributed
into groups and families, genera and species, very
much as naturalists classify animals and plants. Out of
four, or perhaps five, primitive liturgies, there seem to
have been developed an almost countless variety of
forms, each retaining, it is true, a strong family like-
ness to the parent stock, and yet each manifesting
some marked peculiarities of its own. Hence among
the infant sciences "comparative liturgics" claims a
place by the side of comparative philology, and the
proper grouping of liturgies is discussed, like the
proper grouping of languages, with much ability and
earnestness.

But the Anglican *system*, in requiring conformity
to one, and only one liturgy, is manifestly at variance

with the Anglican *principle,* which appeals to primitive
and catholic usage for terms of unity; and since the
present writer is engaged in the advocacy of the Anglican principle alone, it is right that he should confine
himself to the demands of that.

In the Church of the Reconciliation "the Prayer-
book as it is" would doubtless hold its place; and if
that formulary be indeed all that we who love it claim,
there would soon be no competitor in the field. But,
meanwhile, why might there not be congregations
pledged to the four cardinal points which have been
seen to belong to the essence of unity, while yet they
worshipped, some of them with a liturgy modified
from the prevailing type, and some of them with no
liturgy at all, provided there were in this latter case a
guarantee that in the administration of the two Sacraments the words of Christ Himself should be invariably used?

In such an event we certainly should not be further
removed from our fellow Christians of other names
than we now are; on the contrary, we should be much
nearer to them. At any rate, the suggestion ought not
to be condemned without a hearing. The spectacle of
congregations worshipping in different ways while
within the pale of the same church would unquestion-
ably be a novelty; but would it be any more discordant
in the eyes of the God and Father of us all, or any more
scandalous to the mind of an unbelieving world, than
the spectacle which may be seen now of congregations
worshipping in different ways, but *not* within the pale

of the same church? Would not the differences of opinion about the way "men ought to worship," that have been troubling Christians for the last three hundred years, be more likely to disappear if we were to draw the line of our charity *around* the dissentients, than they are if we draw that line *between* these neighbors and ourselves, and then attempt to convert them to our view by talking across the intervening barrier?

The Church of England, no doubt, aimed to remedy a real evil when at the Reformation she declared, in the Preface to her Common Prayer, that "whereas heretofore there hath been great diversity in saying and singing in churches within this realm; some following *Salisbury* Use, some *Hereford* Use, and some the Use of *Bangor,* some of *York,* and some of *Lincoln;* now from henceforth all the whole realm shall have but one Use." But the Acts of Uniformity have not been, in the long run, a distinguished success; and it is just possible that by a more permissive line of legislation we in America can sooner secure the desired result— harmony of worship.[16]

Readers of these papers who have no particular sympathy with Anglican ideas and traditions will wonder, perhaps, at the confidence with which certain points have been urged as absolutely prerequisite to any genuine unity. Churchmen, on the other hand, will many of them wonder far more at the magnitude of the concessions which have been treated as possible.

To the first class of dissentients the whole argument has been addressed, and there is nothing more to urge. To his brother Churchmen the writer would simply say, Consider carefully whether any point has been yielded that is really essential to the Anglican position. This is not a question of preferences, but of principles. Unless we are all of us prepared to accommodate ourselves to what are only the preferences of others, at the same time that we ask them to respect our own, the Church of the Reconciliation may as well be given over at once as a lost cause.

One thing, however, the writer owes it to himself to say. The advocacy or defense of lawlessness has been no part of the purpose of this book. The spirit of insubordination and self-will may raise a storm; it cannot lull one—and it must be remembered that we are now *in* the storm. The love of law is twin sister to the law of love. "Every fringe," says Mgr. Manning, in his stinging rebuke of English Ritualism—"every fringe in an elaborate cope worn without authority is only a distinct and separate act of private judgment; the more elaborate, the less Catholic; the nearer the imitation, the further from the submission of faith."[17] The remark applies in all directions; to those to whom copes are an abomination, and to those who covet copes. The true way to make our Fold catholic is through a generous opening of the gates by the hand of law, not by a promiscuous leaping over the wall at the dictates of individual caprice.

And yet it is perfectly possible for this reverence for law to consist with a passionate longing after a larger measure of practical comprehensiveness than we now see in the Church. The higher a man's Churchmanship in the best sense, that is to say, the more exalted the estimate he holds of the dignity and value of the Church as the Body of Christ, the Pillar and Ground of the Truth, the earthly City of God, all the more eager ought he to be to see the ecclesiastical polity made as elastic and as inclusive as the requirements of holiness and truth will permit. Vastly more than the two adjectives of position, "high" and "low," have we need to dread the two adjectives of quality, "bitter" and "hard." By the phrase "a good Churchman," ought to be intended a Churchman who is good; and a Churchman who is good will love to acknowledge goodness wherever he sees it, and will even go out of his way to find it; for there is no danger of our compromising our Churchmanship by taking large-hearted, as well as large-minded, views upon the great social and religious questions of the day.

If our whole ambition as Anglicans in America be to continue a small, but eminently respectable body of Christians, and to offer a refuge to people of refinement and sensibility, who are shocked by the irreverences they are apt to encounter elsewhere; in a word, if we care to be only a countercheck and not a force in society then let us say as much in plain terms, and frankly renounce any and all claim to Catholicity. We have only, in such a case, to wrap the robe of our dignity about us, and walk quietly along in a seclusion no one will take much trouble to disturb. Thus may we be a Church in name and a sect in deed.

But if we aim at something nobler than this, if we would have our Communion become national in very truth—in other words, if we would bring the Church of Christ into the closest possible sympathy with the throbbing, sorrowing, sinning, repenting, aspiring heart of this great people—then let us press our reasonable claims to be the reconciler of a divided household, not in a spirit of arrogance (which ill befits those whose best possessions have come to them by inheritance) but with affectionate earnestness and an intelligent zeal. We have not, as a communion, such a monopoly of either piety or learning in this land that we can afford to be contemptuous, even if that temper were ever permissible in a Christian Church. But we have, through the blessing of God, the title deeds of the old homestead in our hands; we sit by the hearthstone of the English-speaking race; and ought we to be blamed for thinking that if the family can be gathered anywhere in peace it must be here? Nay, when our fellow Christians tell us that this or that feature of our system is a bar to unity, may we not ask them charitably to consider whether, along with our disadvantages, there be not some advantages not to be found elsewhere, and whether, when the right time comes, it be not just possible that we may have something to contribute towards, as well as something to sacrifice for, the Church of the Reconciliation?

For these reasons it is of the utmost importance to have it known that our real distinction as a Church does not lie, as so many seem to suppose it does, in our preference for pointed architecture, and stained glass, and chanted music, and ministerial vestments, but in our faithful—some will have it obstinate—adherence to the primitive and Catholic standards of unity.

Moreover, let us give the people to understand that we are interested in what interests them. Let us cultivate the power of adaptation to the needs of "all sorts and conditions of men." Let us train our preachers to handle living topics, to throw down the gage to contemporary forms of unbelief, rather than busy themselves with cutting off the heads of deceased giants originally slain by men who had the wit to forge their weapons for themselves. Let us encourage our men of action to head popular movements and direct them, instead of standing daintily aloof,

"In impotence of fancied power."

A rigid, unsympathetic temper on our part will never win America to the Church. We must cause it to be clearly understood that God's Household is large enough and roomy enough for all forms of activity that make for good. The blunders that are conspicuous in the popular crusades of our time and country are largely traceable to the want of that wise guidance which the Church might give, if only she had the confidence and love of the nation. We charge much of the current philanthropy of the day with godlessness. But whose fault is it that this philanthropy is godless? Why, when society feels with unusual pain the pressure of some especial

curse or want, does society look in almost any direction
rather than to the Church for help? Some will answer
that it is because of a certain perverseness in society
itself. This is partly true, but it is not all the truth. We
cannot forget that there was once a time when the
Church was the recognized Mother of beneficence, the
almoner of all tender and gentle charity, the hospital
and asylum and reformatory of the world, as well as the
world's House of Prayer.

Take the temperance movement for example. The
failure of the movement, in so far as it has failed to rid
the community of a frightful curse, has been due to
misdirection. A mistake was committed by the friends
of "the cause" in supposing that banners and proces-
sions and "regalia," and all the accessories of secret
societies, could accomplish what the sacred society
founded long ago in Palestine could not.

And now, after some sixty years of assiduous effort,
and after much making and unmaking of statute law,
men are coming around to the persuasion that in the
old-fashioned principles of mutual help under temptation, and self-denial for a brother's sake, in short, by
putting into practice, each as he has opportunity, the
full Christian law of charity, lies the best hope of the
temperance cause. Yet much failure and disappointment might have been saved had the Church been alive
to the popular need, and made herself a faithful apostle of the true temperance at the start.

Or take another movement which has only just
begun, namely, that in behalf of a larger field of activity

for Women. There is in it much food for easy ridicule. In some of its aspects it is, in truth, what it has been severely called, "a revolt against nature." And yet the movement, with all its crudities and immodesties and extravagances, has a significance which the Church ought not to neglect. These restless souls are not restless wholly without cause; were it so, they would not win a following. The Church has always been woman's best friend in the past; it remains to be seen whether the Church can help woman now, not only by cultivating reverence for those forms of suffering and service which are her appointed lot, but also by opening to her avenues of usefulness, which, if less conspicuous than the Platform and the Bar, are not less sure than they of leading to that honor which is the invariable reward to true desert.

These are but illustrations of the kind of questions which perplex the mind of society. Why is it that the Church of Christ does not grapple with them, and insist on finding an answer? We come back to the old trouble, Disunion. The Church fails, because the Church is broken.

But the horizon is not all overcast. There are many tokens of a golden morning near at hand. People's minds are gradually becoming thoroughly awake to the importance of the subject, and this in itself is a great gain.[18] The first step toward finding a remedy for our ailments is to acknowledge that we are sick. Christendom, with a very querulous voice, is beginning to do just this. Then there is still further encouragement in the fact that all over the world religious thought is concentrating itself more and more every day upon the Person of our blessed Lord. Believers and unbelievers are alike agitated with the question, What think ye of Christ? This is a sure precursor of renewed efforts after unity. The more clearly our holy religion is seen to have its center in Him whose name it bears, the more will those who love Him in sincerity feel that the Church *must* be one.

At any rate, let us who believe in unity hold fast our faith without wavering, well content to rank as fools and mad so long as we are certain that we have the word of Christ and the example of his first missionaries on our side. For be the waves never so angry, the sky never so dark, the forebodings of disaffected friends never so gloomy, if we are confident that the ship's head is right, our only duty is to

"Still bear up and steer Right onward."

Notes

CHAPTER I

The Gospel of the Kingdom

1. The Schoolmen wisely recognized this distinction in their theory of "The Seven Sacraments." Two of the seven, namely, Matrimony and Orders, were held to confer grace on society, as the other five conferred it on the individual. It cannot be denied that a profound truth is latent here.
2. Matt. iv. 23
3. See Bernard's *Progress of Doctrine in the New Testament*, Chap. vii.
4. Some critics prefer the marginal reading " among you," in Luke xvii. 21.

CHAPTER II

The Thought and Its Clothing

1. Luke xxiv. 39.
2. Rev. vii. 9.
3. 1 Cor. i. 1.

4. Much confusion of thought with regard to the Christian doctrine of the Resurrection of the Body would be avoided if this distinction between two sorts of identity—identity of material and identity of growth—were always kept in mind.

CHAPTER III

Romanism: The Idea Exaggerated

1. The issues of the Council of the Vatican are so uncertain that it is folly to attempt to forecast them. In the present paper, therefore, the writer confines himself to the past, not wishing to rest any portion of his argument upon conjectural ground. Whatever Rome may now assert, there are some things she cannot retract. It is with these irreversible steps of hers, already taken, that the critical student is principally concerned. [Original footnote of 1869. W. R. H.]

2. XXXIX Articles, Art. vi.

3. *Ibid.* Art. viii.

4. Well may "Janus" say, in speaking of the possible definition of a "Dogma of the Assumption," "If this floating tradition, too, is made into a dogma, under Jesuit inspiration, it may easily be foreseen that the Order—*l'appétit vient en mangeant*—will bestow many a jewel hereafter on the dogma-thirsting world out of the rich treasures of its traditions and pet theological doctrines."—*The Pope and the Council,* p. 35.

5. The *Eirenicon,* as an Eirenicon, has conspicuously failed. That was a witty saying of the keen-eyed critic of the Oratory, that if his old friend had meant peace, he ought not to have "discharged his olive-branch from a

catapult." And so, it would seem, the issue proves. The "union movement," frozen to death by the coldness of the Vatican, is now only an object of derision, and the *Eirenicon,* after having demonstrated by its contents the impossibility of union upon an Ultramontane basis, now serves to illustrate by its history the hopelessness of union upon a Gallican basis. Viewed in this light, the book has a value that is permanent. Those who are hoping against hope that Rome may yet be persuaded to recognize Anglican Orders, and consent to a capitulation in place of unconditional surrender, will do well to ponder the following utterance of Henry Edward, Archbishop of Westminster: "They who teach that the Anglican separation and the Greek schism are parts of the Catholic Church, violate a dogma of faith, destroy the boundaries of truth and falsehood, and make the blind to wander out of his way."—Manning's *England and Christendom,* p. 68. This is fortified in the appendix to the book quoted by the following official declaration:

"From our letters of Sept. 16, 1864, and Nov. 8, 1865, it is clearly and openly manifest that no one can belong to the true Church of Christ unless he firmly adhere by free subjection of mind and heart and open confession of the lips to the chair of Peter and the Roman Pontiff, who has been divinely constituted by Christ our Lord Himself as successor of Peter, Head of His whole Church, the centre of unity, and Pastor with supreme power of feeding both lambs and sheep. God grant it, venerable brothers, that these unhappy wanderers may abjure their errors, and see the light of Catholic truth, and hasten to the only Fold of Christ. And this we do not omit day and night to ask, in humble and fervent prayers from the Father of Mercies; and for this we again and again implore the powerful patronage of the Immaculate and Most Holy Virgin Mary, the Mother of God."—*Epist. S. D. No Pii. P. IX. ad Episcopos Anglire.* [Footnote of 1869. W. R. H.]

6. The following from Bishop Coxe's Italian letter to Pius IX is not without its force: "You know, besides, that when a council truly ecumenical assembles, its first duty will be to bring a process against you, under the accusation or your equals, the patriarchs of the East, published to the entire Christian world. They accuse you of grave heresies—that is, of having taught from your papal chair, and of having imposed on your followers as *"de fide"* a fable about the blessed *Deipara,* which appears to have had for its sole author Mahomet. You attribute to her the special prerogative of her Divine Son—that is, immaculate conception— in which thing you disturb the very foundations of the faith. That this dogma is altogether contrary to the faith of St. Peter and of his colleagues in the apostleship, and of all the Catholic Church, one of your own doctors, St. Bernard, declares. He called the first intimation of the new dogma *'simplicitas paucorum imperitorum, contra ecclesia ritum, prasumpta novitas, mater temeritatis, soror superstitionis, filia levitatis, quam ritus ecclesia nescit, non probat ratio, non commendat antiqua traditio'* ('the folly of a few fools, a presumptuous novelty, contrary to the usage of the Church, the mother of rashness, the sister of superstition, the daughter of levity, which the rite of the Church knows nothing of, which reason does not approve, nor ancient tradition commend'). Your doctors are accustomed to give to St. Bernard the

title of 'the last of the Fathers'; whence, if St. Bernard had no other knowledge of this dogma, it ought certainly to be unknown to the Fathers before him."— *Mills' Translation.*

7. *The Dogmatic Faith,* The Bampton Lectures for 1867, by the Rev. Edward Garbett, Lect. II.

8. At a book stall in Munich, the writer happened, years ago, upon a little Latin tract apparently intended for the use of seminary students. It bore the title, *"EPITHETA MARIANA ad majorem Dei et B. Maria Virginis honorem ex Scriptura Sacra, Breviario Romano et Litaniis Lauretanis collecta a Xaverio Pfeifer philosophia professore."* A careful count developed the fact that out of the three hundred and eighty-six "epitheta" contained in the collection, *four, and only four,* to wit, "Anoilla Domini," "Benedicta in Mulièribus," "Gratia Plena," and "Virgo desponsata Joseph," were really *"ex Scriptura Sacra."* The rest were from the sources indicated in the title. This is a good illustration of the way in which Rome develops doctrine by "accretion," instead of by "evolution."

9. The careful avoidance by the Roman Catholic authorities of anything that might look like an endorsement of Dr. Newman's *Essay on the Development of Christian Doctrine,* would seem to show that they themselves regard the weapon forged by their most distinguished convert a perilous one to use.

NOTE.—In view of the strenuous effort now making to persuade the American people that Romanism rightly understood is the true remedy for all their social and religious ills, it may not be amiss to reprint, as an English writer has lately done, the famous challenge of old Bishop Jewel and the creed of Pope Pius IV. Neither the challenge nor the creed has ever been retracted, but both remain in force. Not even the rhetoric of Paulist Fathers can bridge the ugly chasm that is here seen to lie between Catholic use and Roman abuse.

Challenge of Bishop Jewel [first made at St. Paul's Cross, Nov. 26, 1559; repeated March 31, 1560].

"If any learned men the articles of all our adversaries, or if all the learned men that be alive, be able to bring any one sufficient sentence out of any old Catholic Doctor or Father, or out of any old General Council, or out of the Holy Scriptures of God, or any one example of the Primitive Church, whereby it may be clearly and plainly proved,

"That there was any private mass in the whole world at that time for the space of six hundred years after Christ; or that there was then any communion ministered unto the people under one kind; or,

"That the people had their common prayers then in a strange tongue that they understood not; or,

"That the Bishop of Rome was then called an Universal Bishop, or the Head of the Universal Church; or,

"That the people was then taught to believe that Christ's Body is really, substantially, corporally, carnally, or naturally in the Sacrament; or,

"That His Body is or may be in a thousand places at one time; or,

"That the Priest did then hold up the Sacrament over his head; or,

"That the people did then fall down and worship it with godly honor; or,

"That the Sacrament was then, or now ought to be, hanged up under a canopy; or,

"That in the Sacrament after the words of consecration there remaineth only the accidents and shows, without the substance of bread and wine; or,

"That the Priest then divided the Sacrament in three parts, and afterwards received himself all alone; or,

"That whosoever had said the Sacrament is a figure, a pledge, a token or a remembrance of Christ's Body had therefore been judged for an heretic; or,

"That it was lawful then to have thirty, twenty, fifteen, ten, or five masses said in one church in one day; or,

"That images were then set up in the churches, to the intent that people might worship them; or,

"That the lay-people was then forbidden to read the Word of God in their own tongue—

"If any man alive were able to prove any of these articles by any clear or plain clause or sentence, either of the Scriptures, or of the old Doctors, or of any old General Council, or by any example of the Primitive Church; I promised them I would give over and subscribe unto him."— Bishop Jewel's *Works*, i.p. 20 (ed. Parker Society).

From *England* versus *Rome*: a Brief Handbook of the Roman Catholic Controversy, for the use of Members of the English Church. By Henry Barclay Swete, M. A. London: Rivingtons.

How theologians like the Abbé Gratry, Dr. Döllinger, and "Janus" (if he be really not the *double* of the Munich Professor), who now so vehemently oppose the definition of the dogma of Infallibility, have reconciled themselves to dogmas which, at the time or promulgation, seemed equally "inopportune," is a standing puzzle to the Protestant mind.

Creed of Pope Pius IV. [imposed A.D. 1564, upon all the beneficed Clergy of the Roman Church].

"I, N., believe and profess with a firm faith each and all of the articles contained in the creed which the Holy Roman Church adopts, to wit:—

"I believe in One God [here follows the 'Nicene Creed.' The Roman form then proceeds.]

"I most steadfastly admit embrace Apostolical and Ecclesiastical Traditions and all other observances and constitutions of the same Church.

"I also admit the Sacred Scriptures, according to that sense which our Holy Mother, the Church, has held and does hold, to which it belongs to judge of the true sense and interpretation of the Holy Scriptures; neither will I ever take and interpret them but according to the unanimous consent of the Fathers.

"I also profess that there are truly and properly seven Sacraments of the New Law, instituted by Jesus Christ our Lord, and necessary for the salvation of mankind, though not for every one; to wit: Baptism, Confirmation, Eucharist, Penance, Extreme Unction, Orders, and Universal Bishop, or the Matrimony; and that they confer grace; and that of these, Baptism, Confirmation, and Orders cannot be reiterated without sacrilege; and I also receive and admit the received approved ceremonies of the Catholic Church, used in the solemn administration of all the aforesaid Sacraments.

"I embrace and receive all and every one of the things which have been defined and declared in Holy Council of Trent, concerning original sin and justification.

"I profess, likewise, that in the Mass there is offered to God a true, proper, and propitiatory sacrifice for the living and the dead; and that in the Most Holy Sacrament of the Eucharist there are truly, really, and substantially, the body, and blood together with the soul and divinity, of our Lord Jesus Christ; and that a conversion is made of the whole substance of the bread into the Body, and of the whole substance of the wine into the Blood, which conversion the Catholic Church calls Transubstantiation. I also confess that under either kind alone, Christ is received whole and entire, and a true Sacrament.

"I constantly hold that there is a Purgatory, and that the souls therein detained are helped by suffrages of the faithful.

"Likewise that the saints reigning together with Christ, are to venerated and invocated; and that they offer prayers to God for us, and that their relics are to be held in veneration.

"I most firmly assert that the images of Christ, of the Mother of God, ever Virgin, and also of other saints, are to be had and retained; and that due honor and veneration are to be paid to them.

"I also affirm that the power of indulgences was left by Christ in the Church, and that the use of them is most wholesome to Christian people.

"I acknowledge the Holy Catholic, Apostolic, Roman Church for the Mother and Mistress of all Churches; and I promise true obedience to the Bishop of Rome, Successor to St. Peter, Prince of the Apostles, and Vicar of Jesus Christ.

"I likewise undoubtedly receive and profess all other things delivered, defined, and declared by the Sacred Canons and General Councils, and particularly by the Holy Synod of Trent; at the same time I condemn, reject, and anathematize all things contrary thereto, and all heresies which the Church has condemned, rejected, and anathematized.

"I, N., do at this present freely profess and sincerely hold this true Catholic faith, without which no one can be saved; and I promise most constantly to retain and confess the same entire and inviolate with God's assistance, to the last breath of life, and I will take care, as far as in me lies, that it shall be held, taught, and preached by my subordinates, that is to say, by those the care of whom shall appertain to me in virtue of my office.

"And this I do promise, vow, and swear: so help me God, and these God's holy Gospels."—*Bullarium*, I. tom. ii. p. 180.

Chapter V

Liberalism: The Idea Distorted

1. St. John viii. 31, 32.
2. Abp. Trench, *The Study of Words, s. v.*
3. The Rev. Edward Everett Hale.
4. It is, of course, by a poetical license that this brilliant, but not always accurate writer makes Canute the Dane a representative of the Heptarchy.
5. *The Elements of Christian Doctrine, and its Development.* Five Sermons preached before the South Congregational Society, Boston, 1860, p. 41.

6. *Ibid.*, p. 40.
7. 1 Pet. iii. 21.
8. *First Annual Report Free Religious Association,* Boston, 1868.
9. John x. 16.
10. The true rendering of John x. 16 undoubtedly requires "one flock," instead of "one fold;" but "flock" suggests limitations almost as much as "fold," and the limitations of Christianity are what make the religion so obnoxious to Liberalism.

CHAPTER VI

The American Problem

1. M. Guizot gives the following compendious summary of the possible relations between Church and State:

"1. The State is subordinate to the Church. In the moral point of view, in the chronological order itself, the Church precedes the State. The Church is the first society, superior, eternal. Civil society is nothing more than the consequence. It is to the spiritual power that sovereignty belongs of right. The temporal power should merely act as its instrument.

"2. It is not the State which is in the Church, but the Church which is in the State. It is the State which rules the land, which makes war, which levies taxes, governs the external destinies of the citizens. It is for the State to give to the religious society the form and constitution which best accord with the interests of general society. Whenever creeds cease to be individual, whenever they give birth to associations, these come within the cognizance and authority of the temporal power, the only veritable power in a State.

"3. The Church ought to be independent, unnoticed in the State. The State has nothing to do with her. The temporal power ought to take no cognizance of religious creeds; it should let them approximate or separate—let them go on and govern themselves as they think best; it has no right, no occasion, to interfere in their affairs.

"4. The Church and the State are distinct societies, it is true; but they are at the same time close neighbors, and are nearly interested in one another. Let them live separate, but not estranged. Let them keep up an alliance on certain conditions, each living to itself, but each making sacrifices for the other in case of need, each lending the other its support."—*Hist. of Civ. in France.* Lect. III.

In the above classification, which seems to be exhaustive, (1) represents the Papal, (2) the Erastian, (3) the American, and (4) the English theory.

2. See a Sermon upon this text, entitled *The Roman Council,* lately preached before the University of Oxford, by the Rev. J. B. Mozley, B. D. The line of thought held in the Sermon is in many respects so like the one followed in this paper that the author feels bound to say that at the time of writing he had not seen any report of Canon Mozley's words.

But even the most clear-headed of English Churchmen, however much they may dislike some features of the Establishment, shrink, with the national dislike of change, from accepting that original status of the Church in which she was utterly and entirely independent of the Civil Power. Thus Canon Mozley guards his strong statements about the distinct scopes and aims

of Church and State with some limiting words against
an absolute separation between the two, and unless Mr.
Gladstone has very recently changed his mind he also,
while standing on the ruins of the Irish Establishment,
still believes in Establishments as desirable under some
circumstances. Here are his words:

"I can hardly believe that even those, including as
they do so many men upright and able, who now con-
tend on principle for the separation of the Church from
the State, are so determined to exalt their theorem to the
place of a universal truth, that they ask us to condemn
the whole of that process, by which, as the gospel spread
itself through the civilized world, Christianity became
incorporated with the action of civil authority, and with
the framework of public law. In the course of human history, indeed, we perceive little of unmixed evil, and far
less of universal good....But Christ died for the race; and
those who notice the limited progress of conversion in
the world until alliance with the civil authority gave to
his religion a wider access to the attention of mankind,
may be inclined to doubt whether, without that alliance,
its immeasurable and inestimable social results would
ever have been attained. Allowing for all that may be
justly urged against the danger of mixing secular motives
with religious administration, and above all against the
intrusion of force into the domain of thought, I for one
cannot desire that Constantine in the government of the
Empire, that Justinian in the formation of its code of
laws, that Charlemagne in re-founding Society, or that
Elizabeth in the crisis of the English Reformation,
should have acted on the principle that the State and the

Church in themselves are separate or alien powers, incapable of coalition."—*A Chapter of Autobiography* by the Rt. Hon. W. E. Gladstone, M. P., pp. 58, 59.

But can Mr. Gladstone deny the truth of the following: "You may bring about many wonderful things through the pliable and elastic constitution of the British Empire, but there is one thing which by its very nature is an impossibility to bring about even by an act of Parliament.

"It is this: That two powers should combine to govern a people in a united religion, which powers themselves are disunited in opinion as to what such religion should be. And especially when one of these powers, holding the sword and virtually having the regulation of the machinery of the other, is in itself composed of an heterogeneous mass of accidental men fluctuating from year to year, and held together by no one bond of faith, not even of Christianity."—*State Interference in Matters Spiritual;* Bennett's Preface to the Fragment by Hurrell Froude.

3. Socialism may perhaps claim to be reckoned a *tertium quid*, the *fraternal* in distinction from the *paternal* theory.

4. Neh. xiii. 2.

5. See Leckey, *History of European Morals,* chap. ii., where this point is brought out with great distinctness.

6. With the possible exception of Russia.

CHAPTER VII
Reconciliation

1. "Where," asks the English Roman Catholic, Edmund Ffoulkes—"where, indeed, is the part of Christendom

seriously purporting to call itself the Catholic Church in these days? Roman Catholic, Anglo-Catholic, Episcopal, Orthodox, or Presbyterian, all in their degree seem influenced by some hidden spell to abstain from arrogating to themselves, or attributing to each other, the epithet of 'Catholic,' without qualification, as it is applied to the Church in the Creed."— *The Church's Creed or the Crown's Creed?* p. 45.

2. Here is the official and definitive language of the Council of Trent: *"Si quis dixerit Baptismum qui etiam datum ab hereticis in nomine Patris et Fili et Spiritus Sancti, cum intentione faciendi quod facit Ecclesia, non esse verum Baptismum, anathema sit."* (Sess. VII., Canon IX.) It is to be regretted that this anathema is sometimes in practice disregarded by those whose consciences it was meant to bind.

3. Nothing is more common than to find these two things confused in people's minds. Perhaps a majority of American Protestants grow up with the notion that admission to the Holy Communion constitutes membership of the Church, and yet the distinction between membership and communion is one that is absolutely essential to a clear understanding of the nature of Church life.

4. *Aids to Faith:* Essay vii. § 12.

5. XXXIX Articles. Art. vi.

6. The date of the Council of Nice was A. D. 325. The closing sentences of the Creed, from the clause "I believe in the Holy Ghost" (with the exception of the words "and the Son"), were added at the Council of Constantinople A. D. 381. Of the Creed thus completed the Fourth General Council (A. D. 451) decreed that it was "lawful for nobody to propose, that is, compile, put together, hold,

or teach others another faith. Those who dared either to put together another faith, or produce, teach, or deliver another symbol to any desirous of returning to a knowledge of the truth from Hellenism, Judaism, or any heresy whatsoever, were, if bishops or clergy, to be deposed; if laymen, to be anathematized."—Canon of Chalcedon, as quoted by Ffoulkes, *The Church's Creed or the Crown's Creed?* p. 5.

Near the end of his pamphlet the same writer says, "Thirdly what is of infinitely more importance to Christians generally, desirous of living in peace and charity with their brethren all the world over, no profession of faith would be required from any seeking to be admitted to communion to any Church, but the Nicene Creed, according to the solemn import of the Canon with which we commenced. When it was passed, all the modern controversies on grace had been anticipated by the followers of Pelagius, and there had been questions raised about the sacraments and rules of the Church similar to those amongst which we live. And still the language of that Canon is most emphatic:—'Those coming over *from whatsoever heresy* to the communion of the Church, are to be made to subscribe to the Nicene Creed and no other.'…Plain Christians might therefore traverse the world with no other passport to the Sacraments of the Church in all lands than the Nicene Creed."—*Ibid.* p. 65.

7. *Ecclesiastical Polity*, Book v. chap. xlii. § 2.
8. *Book of Common Prayer*, Office of Holy Baptism.
9. Not to mention Tract 90, which is now claimed by a not inconsiderable body of Anglican Churchmen as a permissible commentary upon those Articles which it touches. See Dr. Pusey's *Eirenicon*, Part i. p. 30.

10. The writer has left untouched the interesting question as to the present binding authority of the XXXIX Articles upon the clergy of the Protestant Episcopal Church. For light upon this point, he would refer the theological reader to the Journals of the early General Conventions. It is a curious fact that during the first sixteen years of our separate existence as a Church, the XXXIX Articles formed no part of the American Book of Common Prayer; Bishop White, even while defending the Articles *(Memoirs,* p. 240), did "not arrogate to them perpetuity."

11. The writer trusts that he has done the Baptist theology no injustice in these sentences. He does not intend to assert what is practically untrue (although often alleged) that the Baptist system attaches absolutely *no* value to Christian nurture, but rather that Christian nurture is not in that system the prominent feature, the wholly indispensable constituent that is in Anglicanism.

12. *"Nulla Ecclesia sine Episcopo,"* he adds, "has been a fact as well as a maxim since the time of Tertullian and Ireneus."—*Decline and Fall,* vol. i. p. 557, Amer. Ed.

13. In illustration of this, see a profoundly philosophical sermon by Prof. Archer Butler on *Primitive Church Principles not inconsistent with Universal Christian Sympathy.*

14. "The practice of the Episcopal Church in the United States, and now happily introduced in some of our own Colonial Dioceses, in respect of the election of Bishops, seems to approach more nearly than that of any other portion of the Catholic Church to the primitive model described by Cyprian as observed 'fere per universas Provincias.'"—Moberley's *Bampton Lectures* for 1868, p. 333.

15. The following extract is from a most racy and entertaining sermon lately preached by a Congregational clergyman from the text, "*Let another man praise thee, not thine own mouth: a stronger, and not thine own lips.*": "The Episcopal Church offers for our use the most venerable liturgy in the English tongue. The devotional treasures of the Roman Catholic Church are embalmed and buried in Latin. But in English there are no lessons, gospels, psalms, collects, confessions, thanksgivings, prayers-in one word, no religious FORM BOOK that can stand a moment in comparison with the Prayerbook of the Episcopal Church in the twofold quality of richness and age.

"The proper name because truly descriptive, for this Church, would be CHURCH OF THE PRAYER-BOOK. As is the way with all other Churches, so here, the Church champions and leaders have many wise things to say about the Church and her prerogative. But the pious multitude that frequent her courts are drawn thither mostly by love of the prayers and praises, the litanies and lessons of the Prayer-book.

"And, brethren of every name, I certify you that you rarely hear in any church a prayer spoken in English that is not indebted to the Prayer-book for some of its choicest periods.

"And further, I doubt whether life has in store for any of you an uplift so high or downfall so deep, but that you can find company for your soul and fitting words for your lips among the treasures of this Book of Common Prayer."—The Rev. T. K. Beecher, *On the Episcopal Church.*

One can imagine the Puritanism of Booker's time rising from its grave, and exclaiming in dismay to this most undutiful of prophets, "I called thee to curse mine enemies, and behold, thou hast altogether blessed them these three times."

16. It is pleasant to be able to cite in this connection that *clarum et venerabile nomen,* the late Bishop of Maine, George Burgess. He says: "The prayers of the Church maintain, in the judgment of mankind, an almost undisputed supremacy, not only for their venerable antiquity in general, but also as models of doctrinal simplicity, majesty, and fervor. There is in them, confessedly, but the very smallest portion of matter which any believer could hesitate to adopt; and the objections of the Puritan writers amaze the present generation. *But these forms of worship are by no means essential to the existence of that unity which the Episcopate perpetuates.* It is perfectly conceivable that the usages of different communions, their extemporaneous devotions, prayer-meetings, classes, and whatever might have been held conducive to edification, should all be found in churches administered under one Episcopal system."—Bishop Burgess, in the *Bibliotheca Sacra* for October, 1863.

A witness summoned from a very opposite school of thought and practice is the Rev. A. H. Mackonochie, the representative man among the English Ritualists. At the Liverpool Church Congress he contended for perfect liberty, especially in the framing of short services. In particular, he instanced the case of working men, who were too tired, after their day's work, for regular Even-song:

"At such a time a few solemn readings of Holy Scripture—merely a few verses, which they could remember and take away with them, of encouragement, admonition, or warning, as the priest or clergyman might see fit—with perhaps one or two hymns, would be of immense value to them. And he did not see why, if souls could be saved by extempore prayer, they should not have extempore prayer. The question was not satisfying this person or that person; it was not the carrying out of a rigid system, but it was the laying hold of souls for their blessed Lord's sake. If one section of the Church—those who agreed mostly with him—thought that by such occasional services they could best fulfill their duty, let them have them. And if there were others who thought that by extempore prayer, in one form or other, they could best lay hold of their own people, he for one also said, why should they not have them? (Cheers.)

"Mr. Mackonochie stated that while in Scotland last summer he had been invited to conduct a service in a fisherman's hut on the Presbyterian model. He complied, and so far as he could tell, the poor people entered heartily into the service; it did them good, as it certainly did him." (Loud applause.)

17. *England and Christendom,* Introduction, p. lxxxiii.

18. Even while these last pages are passing through the press, the writer's attention has been called to a new treatise on this subject from the pen of the Rev. Dorus Clark, D.D., a Congregational clergyman. Dr. Clark writes upon *The Oneness of the Christian Church,* and nothing could be more pronounced or vigorous than his exposure of the fallacies of sectarianism. Christ

intended, he insists, not merely a spiritual fellowship among his followers, but an actual and visible oneness: a Church unity over and above a Christian unity.

But from this height of premise Dr. Clark presently falls to what the writer, with the convictions he has already expressed as to the necessity of an historical basis of unity, cannot but regard as a most unsatisfactory conclusion. Dr. Clark sees no hope of Church unity save as it may emerge out of a better understanding than has ever yet existed among theologians with regard to the right interpretation of the Scriptures. The recent advances in Biblical science warrant, he thinks, the expectation that such a *Consensus* may yet be attained. But it is difficult to see how this conclusion consists with what is said in the earlier part of the same treatise about the folly of expecting Church unity to be brought about by a convention of denominations. How otherwise could it be brought about, when the need of historical continuity has been once repudiated? Why not rather take the primitive Creeds as the only Biblical *consensus* necessary, and then make unity actual, as well as ideal, through the Sacraments and the Episcopate? But while thus dissenting from what seems to him the inconsequence of Dr. Clark's argument, the writer may be permitted to express his warm admiration of *The Oneness of the Christian Church*, as a bold protest against what has been the too common line of teaching with writers upon American ecclesiastical polity. Among "the signs of the times" in New England, the book claims a conspicuous place.